100 GREAT CHINESE POSTERS

**Recent examples of "the people's art"
from The People's Republic of China**

Stewart E. Fraser

IMAGES GRAPHIQUES, INC. New York

THE POSTER ART LIBRARY

Edited by Jack Rennert

Already published:
100 YEARS OF BICYCLE POSTERS • 100 YEARS OF CIRCUS POSTERS
100 YEARS OF DANCE POSTERS • 100 YEARS OF MAGIC POSTERS
100 POSTERS OF BUFFALO BILL'S WILD WEST
100 YEARS OF POSTERS OF THE FOLIES-BERGÈRE AND MUSIC HALLS OF PARIS
100 POSTERS OF PAUL COLIN

In preparation:
100 GREAT FILM POSTERS • 100 SAN FRANCISCO ROCK POSTERS
100 STUDENT PROTEST POSTERS • 100 YEARS OF OPERA POSTERS
PAL: 100 GREAT POSTERS OF THE BELLE EPOQUE
THE STROBRIDGE SAGAS: 100 POSTERS OF THE THEATRE OF MELODRAMA
100 YEARS OF TRAVEL POSTERS • 100 POSTERS OF CELESTINO PIATTI
100 POSTERS OF WALDEMAR SWIERZY • 100 POSTERS OF GUNTHER KIESER
100 POSTERS OF JULES CHERET • 100 POSTERS OF TADANORI YOKOO

STEWART E. FRASER is one of the world's leading authorities in the field of comparative international education. He is presently at the School of Education of La Trobe University, Victoria, Australia, where he holds the Chair of Education in the Centre for Comparative & International Studies in Education. Previously he served as Professor of International and Comparative Education and Director of the International Center at the George Peabody College for Teachers, Nashville University Center, from 1963 to 1975. Before that he had served as Assistant Director of the International Office, Harvard University, and was a Research Associate at the Harvard Graduate School of Education.

Professor Fraser has taught as visiting lecturer variously in the United States at the University of Colorado, University of Wyoming, Tennessee Technological University, Vanderbilt University, University of Virginia, University of California at Los Angeles, as well as the University of Melbourne, Hiroshima University, Kyoto University, Academy of Pedagogical Sciences U.S.S.R., University of Calgary, University of British Columbia, University of Copenhagen and the University of Oslo.

He holds the Doctor of Education degree from the University of Colorado in higher education, and the Doctor of Philosophy degree in historical and comparative studies in education from the University of London. In addition, Professor Fraser has studied at Melbourne, Stanford and Oxford universities for degrees in social sciences and education.

Professor Fraser has served on the editorial board of and contributed to many leading journals in the field of international education; he was a research consultant to various departments and ministries of education, in the United States, Brazil, Iceland and other countries; and he served as chairman of Phi Delta Kappa's Commission on International Relations in Education.

Of the more than twenty books he has authored in the field of comparative international education, only a few can be cited here: *A History of International and Comparative Education: Nineteenth Century Documents* (co-editor, Scott, Foresman & Co: Glenview, Ill., 1968); *American Education in Foreign Perspectives: Twentieth Century Essays* (John Wiley & Sons: New York, 1969); *A Study on North Korean Education Under Communism Since 1945* (co-author, Peabody International Center, U.S. Office of Education: Nashville, 1969); *Chinese Communist Education: Records of the First Decade* (Vanderbilt University Press: Nashville, 1965; John Wiley & Sons, 1966); *Chinese Education and Society: A Bibliographic Guide; The Cultural Revolution and Its Aftermath* (co-author, International Arts and Sciences Press: New York, 1972); *Education and Communism in China: An Anthology of Commentary and Documents* (Pall Mall Press: London, 1970); *Governmental Policy and International Education* (John Wiley & Sons: New York, 1965); *Research in International Education, 1966-67* (co-author, Institute of International Education: New York, 1967); *Sex, Schools & Society: International Perspectives* (Aurora Publishers, Inc.: Nashville & London, 1972). He is presently completing *The Young Face of China*, a book of photographs taken during his many visits to The People's Republic of China.

Editor's Acknowledgments

As with all other books in this series, this volume represents the collaborative effort and the helping hand of many individuals. We are grateful to all of them, although only a few can be mentioned here.

All posters in The Poster Art Library are photographed directly from the original posters and therefore a good photographer is one of the most essential elements; for this book we were fortunate to have one of the very best, Mr. Martin Jackson. From there, color separation was carefully handled by Mr. Kanae Akiyama of Daiichi Seihan, assisted by Mr. Tomeji Maruyama. The design and layout was under the supervision of Mr. Harry Chester, assisted by Mr. Alexander Soma of his staff. Typography was handled with efficiency by Brandy Stevens of Popular Typography. Printing was provided with great care and personal attention by the staff of MacNaughton Lithograph and Command Web Offset; I am especially indebted to Mr. Andrew Merson and Mr. Gary Feller. And the staff of Images Graphiques helped in countless ways: special thanks are due to Ms. Helen Garfinkle, Mr. Chester Collins and Mr. Stu Solow.

—Jack Rennert
Editor,
The Poster Art Library

IMAGES GRAPHIQUES, INC.
37 Riverside Drive
New York, New York 10023

Library of Congress Catalog Card Number: 77-94467

ISBN (Softcover) 0-89545-007-0
ISBN (Hardcover) 0-89545-006-2

First Printing, November 1977

Printed in the United States of America

Introduction

The posters included in this collection represent but a modest sample of the enormous outpouring of works currently produced by Chinese artists and posterists. Moreover, the collection reflects the interest of one particular individual, and although a range of styles, media and themes is demonstrated, it does not claim to be thematically complete or representative of all the major artistic styles. However it makes claims to relevancy and recency as the posters reflect some of the major facets of contemporary Chinese society. They have been gathered during a number of visits to China during the past few years and represent a significant portion of the author's collection. A number of perhaps equally relevant and similarly illustrative items have not been included for the obvious reason of space. Some items have been incorporated, not because of high aesthetic appeal, but rather as an illustration of art styles popular in China.

Poster art in China has recently blossomed in a widening range of styles and thematic representations, to an extent not seen in previous decades. It could even be argued that Chinese poster art is at its highest point in terms of both versatility and artistic license since the first establishment of the People's Republic in 1949. The range of subject matter has undoubtedly expanded from the somewhat narrow and exclusive portrayals of the 1950's and 1960's to the more imaginative works of greater amplitude seen in the late 1970's.

Poster design, production, and distribution in China has certain obvious political constraints when compared with the generally commercialized, often individualized, approach to posters characteristic of the West. There is perhaps a problem of both aesthetic and political relevance for the foreigner who looks at Chinese posters and sees them in terms of the kind of political art which normally emanates from his own country. It needs to be emphasized that mass-produced poster art in China is a controlled medium, and though there is an increasing number of works appearing which do not have an obvious or total political message, the initiation, commissioning, production, and dissemination of poster art is the acknowledged political responsibility of the government, expressed in the collective action of different levels of workers and various committees.

Some of the items in this collection are more normally intended for internal consumption by the Chinese and have been obtained by the author during various visits to China. Others are available from overseas distributors, and some have been intended by the Chinese specifically for an international audience. This, in some cases, may be noted by the multilingual captions often written in English, French, Spanish, and German. The distribution of Chinese poster art throughout the world has contributed to the popularization both of the medium and the message of revolutionary action to an extent which may have even surprised the Chinese themselves.

This particular collection does not claim to portray all the artistic styles or techniques and the myriad of themes popularized by the Chinese posterist. But it does lay claim to providing at least a basic visual synopsis of some of the current political activities and social moods of China as seen through the eyes of many talented artists. The past decade has produced posters of varied style to encompass the themes of the Great Proletarian Cultural Revolution, the struggle against imperialism and colonialism, patriotism and defense of the motherland, expansion of agriculture, development of industry, and the recognition of humble heroes who "serve the people". Posters with a political or social realism theme predominate, but there are items which have a more purely aesthetic appeal and which perhaps could even be described as almost apolitical. The joyful and harmonious New Year posters wishing long life and national prosperity, the idyllic pastoral scenes illustrating the beauty and grandeur of the Chinese countryside, are all available in poster form for the masses to enjoy. The cost of purchasing posters is but a few cents; however, the available range changes with the political climate.

The use of posters in China, whether for commercial advertising or political haranguing, is certainly not a recent innovation dating, as some might believe, from the inception of the Communist government and the proclamation of the People's Republic in 1949. The history of modern Chinese poster art has its genesis in the 1920's and 1930's, and though the results may not compare in volume, distribution or reproduction quality with today's products, their hoped for impact and audience are still the same—namely the Chinese masses—a people who were perhaps less than a third literate barely half a century ago. The highly colored illustrative poster was perhaps one of the most apt mediums for a population which was generally illiterate, spoke in various regional dialects, and was faced with the enormous problems of understanding ideograms without the benefit of a simplified phonetic alphabet.

But the intervening quarter of a century, since 1949, has seen the virtual elimination of illiteracy, especially amongst young people, the growth of a simplified and more readable system of ideogram–characters, and the parallel introduction of a latinized alphabet with phonetic spelling. All these factors have contributed to increasing the level of mass understanding. Literacy rates of over eighty percent are now being claimed for the total population in China. Certainly the younger generation under fifteen years, or a third of the total population, would be closer to ninety percent literate after completing primary school.

The increasing standards of literacy have not in any way diminished the importance of the vivid and illustrated poster. To the contrary, the poster with the visual message is more often complemented with appropriate slogans or text for added impact.

The popular saying "one picture is worth a thousand words" is of Chinese origin. Hence, the use of vivid posters to deliver messages to the masses comes naturally to the Chinese. Actually, several communicative elements—pictures, words, films, slogans, and posters—are used jointly and interchangeably in China today. The political poster flamboyantly proclaims the current slogans in vogue just as the paintings, in traditional art style, are employed to convey both aesthetic messages and ideological injunctions. The poster in New China is both the medium and the message whose presence, while taken for granted now by the masses, is a recurrent visual notation accepted, understood, and appreciated by virtually all. The use of the political poster in China, whether to proclaim the "Smashing of Confucius and Lin Piao" or "Elimination of the Gang of Four" is often a colorful visual expression of the latest ideological line to be followed by the Chinese masses. But ideological posters espousing the current party line are certainly not the only ones to which the artist addresses himself.

Today, with a "hundred flowers blooming" almost any subject, if approved, and virtually most artistic mediums, if recognized, may be included for mass production and distribution. A painting can be quickly popularized, and through a poster format, may be available for national, if not international, distribution. The delicate brush and ink artistry and multicolored woodblock prints compete with each other for attention. Some posters are initiated and designed to be distributed specifically as a mass product from their first inception. Others start out in a small exhibit in a village or a commune art collection. Their life can be extended and status elevated by appropriate political and cultural recognition. Through the offices of various regional publishing houses, paintings are selected for reproduction as prints and/or posters and accordingly become eligible for wider distribution. Some posters in mass production obviously have little claim on popular appeal and, as in other societies, may be more purely of an instructional or educational nature. Others are destined for a specific distribution, particularly those promoting for example "factory safety" or "public hygiene." Some are for classroom or institutional use and incorporate visual materials normally required as teaching aids in, say, physics, geography, anatomy, or acupuncture classes. Technical posters of this nature, while informative and educational, are omitted from this collection unless they have something specific to say regarding Chinese usage and employment.

This collection focuses on themes and artistic styles which portray the contemporary Chinese scene in as many forms as possible. Thus gouaches, oils, water colors, brush and ink drawings, and woodblock prints are all included where the artist's work is translated ultimately into the lithographic poster art form. The range of subjects includes the sensitive renderings of beautiful southern river panoramas such as those of the Hsi Chiang or the dry, expansive, sparse brown Mongolian pastures of the Silingol Grasslands. Posters depicting natural beauty are interspersed with works focusing on man-made irrigation projects and industrial subjects.

Perhaps it is the more identifiable and dynamic poster involving human action and political interaction that catches best the moment of the political scene. Over two-thirds of the posters in this collection involve some form of direct human action, and nearly half of these relate to the political behavior and ideological activity of the kind which one comes to expect in a country such as China.

It should come as no surprise to find that politically inspired posters from China are sometimes featured on the front covers of international journals. The themes and artistic styles of Chinese posterists are of such nature that they often make appealing and thought provoking covers. Such relevant examples of this usage can be seen in the case of various recent publications intended for world-wide distribution. One recent journal from China utilizes a vivid poster titled "Denounce the Gang of Four Anti-party Clique for Plotting to Seize Party and State Power". It shows, in heroic pose, representatives of Chinese workers, peasants, and soldiers, both men and women, attacking Wang Hun-wen, Chang Chun-chiao, Chiang Ching (Mao Tse-tung's widow) and Yao Wen-yuan. The poster appears in the February-March, 1977 edition of *China Reconstructs*. Another Chinese poster appeared recently in *People,* the quarterly of the International Planned Parenthood Federation, London. The poster, which appeared in the Summer issue for 1975, highlights the Chinese saying that "Wo-

men hold up half the Sky". This particular issue is devoted entirely to family planning programs and women's activities in China. Chinese posters have also found their way irregularly into various foreign specialist publications during the past few years, including, for example, the respected American education journal, *Phi Delta Kappan*. In April 1972 and in April 1975, it published articles on foreign education and used in these cases appropriate Chinese posters for its front covers.

As in any other collecting, there are degrees of rarity. The most commonly available posters are mass-produced in numerous publishing houses found in major cities or in provincial centers. Unfortunately, many imaginative posters one sees while travelling in China represent the "one of a kind" variety, either produced by an individual for a street community, or perhaps a group of children for their school notice board. The prolific production of such individual posters, while indubitably an important part of the Chinese scene, is beyond the scope of this collection. Quite a few highly individualistic, controversial, and polemical posters are of this unique genre, and unfortunately pass away with all too rapid frequency, without being recorded for posterity. Similarly, the gargantuan "one of a kind" billboards which occupy prominent places in the thoroughfares of major Chinese cities are also outside the purview of this book. Instead, this collection focuses on mass-produced, commercially available material. This caveat is perhaps necessary to dispel the notion that the contents of this

book represents the full range of poster art as seen in China today.

The reader is also reminded that posters in this particular collection have also undoubtedly passed the review of a hierarchy of committees, censors, and review boards before final publication and ultimate dissemination. However, the change of political wind, and the vagaries of ideological climate, place some "officially" produced posters all too quickly beyond the pale and make them "unacceptable to the masses". They obviously become, in a Western sense, collectors' items, but *memorabilia non grata* from the viewpoint of Communist Party officialdom. Discredited leaders are moved from an honored central position in a poster to become, on the periphery, figures of derision and ridicule. An example is that of Lin Piao, formerly "a close comrade-in-arms of Chairman Mao", who in the space of a few years has been rotated a hundred and eighty degrees to become the "arch enemy of the Chinese people, in league with Confucius". The recent exposure and repudiation of the "Gang of Four" is perhaps the latest example, illustrated so graphically in poster art, of the vagaries of Chinese political fortunes. The total destruction of the public image of Chiang Ching, the fourth wife of Mao Tse-tung, as the leading member of the "Gang of Four", likewise has occurred within the space of a year after his death. The current works, being publicly affixed throughout China, attest to the use of the poster medium as the most visible and powerful sign of denigration for those who "attempt to usurp power".

Themes Recurrent and Perennial

Themes portrayed in this collection may be grouped for convenience under a variety of headings such as those reflecting either aesthetics, politics, education, etc. But they all represent some particular aspect of Chinese society depicted during the 1970's. Some reflect the political and social values currently eschewed by the government or relive an historical incident in modern Chinese history. Certain themes continually recur and are revitalized with each successive portrayal.

Mao Tse-tung

It is to be expected, and the average Chinese would not have it otherwise, that Chairman Mao is to be portrayed as the central figure who receives the greatest personal recognition. If Mao is not identified in person, his "thoughts", "writings", or "quotations" are presented symbolically either through the clear identification of his Little Red Book or in a prominently displayed pertinent slogan (22, 76, 86, 100, 108, 110, 111).

Because Chairman Mao as a centerpiece is a well known poster subject, this collection includes only a limited number in which he is featured. A representative example is "New Year in Yenan" (96), with Mao surrounded by

children, villagers and soldiers in a scene depicting the festive gathering during the winter in the early 1940's. "March Forward for the Great Proletarian Cultural Revolution" (99) celebrates a major movement in the late 1960's; "Relationship Between a Teacher and Pupil is as Close as a Family" (19) features Mao as the teacher of children; "Express with Words" (18) suggests the scholar, writer, poet, educator and theoretician at work in the early, formative period of his life, the twenties.

Folk Heroes

A regime based on the Marxist doctrine of dictatorship of the proletariat needs, in addition to great leaders, also great models from the ranks of ordinary people with whom the average person could identify. One needs only to be reminded of the great build-up given by the Soviet propaganda machine in the 1920's to Stakhanov, the obscure miner who in one shift dug some twenty times the amount of coal that was the norm at the time.

The Chinese have gone the same route with several such new style heroes and even entire model communities. Lei Feng (37, 61) was a truck driver for the Army when he was killed at the age of 22 in the line of duty. At the personal request of Mao, he was posthumously elevated to the stature of a hero for youth to emulate.

Other new heroes of this type include Tong Tsung-jui (16), Wu Ye-tao (21), and Tong Tsu (66.)

Recognition in this collection is also afforded the highly respected and revered late premier Chou En-lai (107) and already a number of posters noting his contributions have appeared on the anniversary of his death, January 8, 1976.

Place names that have a deep meaning in new China include some of the symbols of the Communist struggle of the past, such as Yenan (34, 97) which was the headquarters of Mao Tse-tung's ragtag guerilla army for many years, and Shao Shan (68), Mao's birthplace. Very prominent play is given in all Chinese propaganda media to Tachai (29, 45, 46, 96, 108, 112), a village chosen to represent the kind of progress that can be made if all members of a community pull together to improve their lives.

Internationalism

Internationalism in its many forms is a favorite theme and is exemplified in "Long Live the Proletariat" (22) which celebrates the hundredth anniversary of the Paris Commune; "Revolutionary Friendships are Deeper than the Oceans" (23) that depicts African visitors viewing the Chinese-made tractor with the brand-name of 'Shanghai'; and "Long Live the United People of the

World" (24) which places revolutionaries of the world in review for inspection. Chinese posters with an international focus have skillfully employed the themes of anti-colonialism, anti-imperialism, and the solidarity of the Chinese people with third-world countries involved in military and political struggles. Poster 94 illustrates the violent nature of the struggle of African peoples. Other posters published in China (not illustrated in this collection) have identified with the wartime resistance of Vietnam, civil rights struggles of blacks in the United States, and solidarity with Albania, China's erstwhile "European Ally and Western Bridgehead".

Defense

The border disputes with the Soviet Union have, for over a decade, occupied an important place in poster propaganda, and "Iron Bastion, Joint Defense By the Army and the People" (101) illustrates this point. The scene depicts three soldiers on the northern borders prepared to repel invaders.

Posters depicting the downing of U.S. spy aircraft over South China seen in juxtaposition with posters emphasizing the dictum "We shall Liberate Taiwan", have been regular features of the past decade. Although not politically muted today in print or verbal rhetoric, these have perhaps occupied less prominence in the current poster scene. However, the need for military preparedness in the Taiwan straits and coastal defense are featured in two posters in the collection, namely "Coastline Defense" (35), and "Willing to Come When Called" (105).

The defense of the motherland, the military readiness of the Chinese people, the integration of regular army and local militia, and the mutual support of civilian factory irregulars and professional soldiers are topics illustrated vividly in the poster medium. In this collection, for example, the mutual cooperation between civilian militia, peasants, and the Peoples Liberation Army is featured in posters 22, 83, 102, 106, and 109. The preparedness and aggressive training of the army in basic military skills is featured in posters 33, 35, 36, 37, 101, 103, and 104.

Minorities

Many of the posters illustrate the presence of numerous minority people who are found throughout China. The recognized fifty-four national or ethnic groups include the Tibetans, Uighers, Kazakhs, Thai, Jiao-Mios, Koreans, and Mongolians. See, for example, posters 26, 31, 32, 68, 69, 72, 95, 101, 104, 111 and 112.

Women

The role of women in all walks of life—ranging from tractor mechanic to mounted militia—is a constant and major theme. Work that men traditionally had undertaken in China is now clearly identified with tasks and roles that women are expected to participate in alongside men in a spirit of comradely co-operation. The equality of personal opportunity is linked to the equality of service to the state. The mining of coal represents one of the tasks normally reserved for men and "A

Newcomer to the Mine" (39) illustrates a woman miner reporting for duty. This poster, which has enjoyed much popularity for nearly five years, appeared first as an oil painting, was printed as a large scale poster, and then appeared in print collections, calendars, and even as the design for a postage stamp. It is perhaps one of the most widely distributed posters which reflects the genre of women's liberation. Almost a third of the items in the collection examine the role of women in modern Chinese society and illustrate the obvious and conscientious effort of the posterist and government to highlight the new and enhanced role of women. Some themes illustrate women at work in areas perhaps more traditionally associated with their sex, such as herb collecting (73), and the rural doctors, nurses, and medical workers (71, 72, 93). Perhaps it should be noted here that Chinese sexual attitudes do not reflect, as in most Western countries, commercial conditioning and advertising which shows the superiority and domination of the male. To the contrary, women of all types, ages, and races are portrayed as entirely equal to men. The theme of the equality of the sexes "cooperating, cohabiting, and coworking" serves as a ubiquitous model for all forms of public advertising. But not a hint of sexuality is present; it is our social awareness which is aroused.

Peasant Paintings

A number of items in the collection come from the well known Peasant Paintings of Huhsien County, Shensi Province, and includes "Spring Cultivation" (30), "Brigade Chicken Farm" (55), "Brigade's Ducks" (54), "Old Party Secretary" (81), and "Today's Foolish Old Men Create New Scenes", (56). The themes are entirely agricultural and involve working people as peasants mastering their own environment. The paintings are universally optimistic, generally dynamic and flow from daily real life situations. Colors are generally strong and bright. The painting techniques would be, by some schools, classified as primitive, natural, unpretentious, and certainly "concrete". A Westerner might appreciate the impressionistic style in posters 54 and 55. The Chinese would perhaps phrase it somewhat differently and place it within an ideological framework, as noted at the time of Huhsien County Paintings exhibit:

"Most of the county's amateur artists had drunk deeply of the bitterness of the old society. Hence they have an especially strong sense of the happiness of life in the new. Their works breathe furious condemnation of the old order. They sing the praises of the Communist Party and Chairman Mao, who led the peasants to stand up and liberate themselves, and of the new socialist countryside and the new life . . . The Huhsien peasants are not engaged in "art for art's sake". They use their brushes as powerful weapons in revolutionary struggle . . . With their rich experience of life, Huhsien's amateur art-

ists produce works that are vivid, natural and unaffected. Persons they paint have clearcut individual characteristics. When they present scenery, whether towering mountains or flowing streams, crisscrossing power lines or field ridges, the treatment is realistic and straightforward. They portray life with deep insight and sensitive perception."

In the past fifteen years the Peasants of Huhsien county have been credited with producing over 40,000 art works, which take the form of wall paintings (murals), New Year pictures, picture story series, papercuts, woodcuts, and paintings in traditional style, gouaches and oils. These have been displayed first through blackboard and wall newspapers, mobile shows, lantern slides, and small scale exhibitions. The fame of the Huhsien paintings has spread, and selections of these works have been sent abroad in traveling exhibitions.

New Year Posters

Several of the posters in the collection are illustrative of one of the more popular genre of Chinese art, namely the "Nien Hua" or New Year picture. This has been a centuries old observance long popular throughout China, particularly in the countryside. The New Year posters and associated art work decorate the home and are found on the walls, windows, cupboards, and ceilings during the advent of the Lunar New Year now more popularly recognized as the 'Spring Festival'. Colors such as red, blue, green, and yellow predominate. Traditionally the posters were the result of multi-colored woodcut printing techniques, though today offset-lithography is used for mass production. The Chinese describe their New Year, or Spring Festival, posters as "a powerful means for spreading new ideas, breaking down old customs and helping to consolidate the dictatorship of the proletariat". New Year posters in this collection include "A Thousand Songs and a Million Dances for the Communist Party" (111), "New Year in Yenan" (97), and "Peasants and Workers Greeting the New Year" (51).

Political Propaganda

The Political Propaganda poster as a modifier and a recreator of instant visual history for mass consumption is a political fact of life in China today. The poster often fulfills a critical role in the public realignment, reorientation, and reordering of political priorities. "Instant history" posters illustrate in vivid, unmistakable form the attack on certain key persons when they fall from official favor, such as Liu Shao-chi, Lin Piao, and Chiang Ching (100, 108). Historical figures from China's past likewise may be appropriate targets for the posterist as exemplified by the recent and continuing ideological compaign against Confucius (100).

The poster can just as easily usher in a new symbolic relationship and a change of political realities. Such a work of major political importance which focuses on the relationship of Mao Tsetung and Hua Kuo-feng has just been completed.

The viewer of Chinese poster art perhaps should be reminded that mass-produced posters, or for that matter any other form of art and literature produced in China today, is expected to follow certain ideological canons laid down by Mao Tse-tung over thirty-five years ago. In a series of talks delivered at a symposium in the Communist headquarters of Yenan, Northwest China, in May, 1942, Mao made a speech, now published as *The Yenan Forum on Literature and Art*.

The guidelines then formulated have been followed in succeeding years with varying degrees of intensity and have been subject to considerable political interpretation and reinterpretation by various power groups in China. The *Yenan Forum* document indicates some of the parameters to be observed in developing art forms which are both indigenous and Communist, in order to enhance the cultural consciousness of the Chinese masses. Mao Tse-tung's political philosophy as applied to art may be best summarized in an often quoted portion of his famous speech:

"In the world today all culture, all literature and art belong to definite classes and are geared to definite political lines. There is in fact no such thing as art for art's sake, art that stands above classes or art that is detached from or independent of politics. Proletarian literature and art are part of the whole proletarian revolutionary cause; they are, as Lenin said, cogs and wheels in the whole revolutionary machine."

Chinese Posters: How to Obtain Them

An obvious and perhaps most rewarding way of building up a poster collection is to visit China and obtain material in person. Alternatively, one can ask a friend traveling to China to purchase posters at the special print and poster shops or at art counters found in leading department stores located in most major Chinese cities.

Another way is to order the posters from the numerous China publication bookshops located abroad which act as the official disbributors of Chinese government materials. The majority of these import bookshops stock a range of Chinese posters.

The devotee of such material who cannot either visit China in person or obtain the posters through a foreign book distributor may instead avail himself of the excellent facsimile prints now available in portfolio editions. This is a popular and inexpensive way of building up a collection of poster prints although perhaps not as visually or aesthetically satisfying as the genuine article. The portfolio print editions of Chinese posters now available include *Peasant Paintings from Huhsien County* published by the Fine Arts Collection Section of the Cultural Group, State Council (1974), *Shantung Art Selections* (To commemorate the Thirtieth Anniversary of Chairman Mao's Speech in Yenan on Literature and Art) published by the People's Fine Art Publishing House, Peking (1974), and *All China Art Collection: Chinese Art Exhibition: Selections from Chinese Art* published by the People's Fine Art Publishing House, Peking (1973).

If a local seller of Chinese publications is unable to assist it would be advisable to write directly to Guozi Shudian, China Publications Centre, P.O. Box 399, Peking, People's Republic of China requesting information concerning either standard size posters or poster-prints collections available for sale abroad.

In addition it may be worthwhile to subscribe to some of the Chinese periodicals which regularly publish articles concerning Chinese art, including paintings and poster material. Three such periodicals specifically provide coverage on the latest pictorial works of Chinese artists which invariably represent a variety of art styles. They include *China Pictorial,* a large-size magazine published monthly in sixteen languages, including English, French, German, Spanish, and Italian; *China Reconstructs,* an illustrated monthly of medium size which provides a general coverage on China published in five languages including English, French, and Spanish; and *Chinese Literature,* the principal periodical dealing with literature and art which is in small size and is published monthly in English and French.

Bibliographical Notes

All of the above periodicals provide coverage of the Chinese art scene, with *Chinese Literature* providing a regular feature on contemporary art often relating directly to paintings and poster production. For the guidance of readers who subscribe to these journals listed above or those who may have access to them or similar periodicals on China, the following brief bibliographical notes may be of interest.

S. Marie Carson: "Dialogue on the Peasant Art of Huhsien," *Eastern Horizons,* Vol. XIII, No. 5, 1974, pp. 7-22.
————: "The National Art Exhibition of 1977," *China Reconstructs,* Vol. XXVI, No. 7, July 1977, pp. 11-14.
Chi Cheng: "National Art Exhibition," *Chinese Literature,* No. 3, 1977, pp. 98-102.
————: "The Oil Painting 'Chairman Mao with the Anyuan Miners'," *Chinese Literature,* No. 7, 1977, pp. 105-107.
————: "Soldiers Art," *China Reconstructs,* Vol. XXV, No. 8, August 1976, pp. 40-44.
————: "Children Love Painting and Drawing," *China Reconstructs,* Vol. XXV, No. 6, June 1976, pp. 32-35.
Hung Lu: "Some Outstanding Peasant Paintings," *Chinese Literature,* No. 3, 1977, pp. 98-102.
Li Feng Jan: "How I Began to Paint the Countryside," *China Reconstructs,* Vol. XXIII, No. 1, January 1974, pp. 21-23.

Editor's Notes

If there is an ambivalence on the part of a Westerner towards China, then, to this writer—who has never traveled there—the posters from The People's Republic of China shown in this collection do little to assuage such feelings. They are frequently compelling, the graphics are often vivid, but at the same time they are absolutely frightening in their pervasiveness: They are unremittingly an instrument and reflection of total political control. And the posters shown here are only a part of the arsenal of concentrated propaganda, reinforced through all other available media and educational channels. All this evidence of the unlimited collective power to manipulate media and the people who are its servants should therefore be a most oppressive sight to us. But what is surprising—and what is possibly the strength of these posters—is that in spite of this they fascinate us and hold our attention—if not always our full respect and understanding.

What saves the day is the brilliance of the colors and very directness of approach: Much of it has the simplicity and boldness of comic art, but much also has embellishments and refinements of design and composition that elevate it, sometimes quite far above the mundane.

The bright colors, often in the richness of clothing (26, 31, 69, 97) or scenery (55, 57, 63) turn otherwise dull posters into compelling works. And the design, though appearing simplistic at times, is, in fact, quite deliberate and, in many cases, quite effective. In addition to such already-classical works as The Fish Pond (53), The Brigade's Ducks (54) and the Brigade Chicken Farm (55), one can note attention to design elements in many other posters as well: The counting lesson at the market (70) would be yet-another-happy-grouping, but for the fact that the people are framed by beautifully arranged and lusciously-colored vegetables; the apple-pickers on their way to work would be just another happy-to-toil-group, if not for the decorative, almost ornamental, use of richly colored fruit (77).

The single most critical thing to be said about these posters, from the point of design, is that they are static: there are few dramatic posters. Could this be a case of detente dampening the anti-imperialist spirit of the posterist? Probably not, but the fact is that there is little real drama or movement in the 1970's posters from China. War cries are patently war games (103) and even when we are urged to resolutely support the struggle against colonialism, it is a statue—heroic but impotent—which urges us on (94). The way the Chinese artist gets movement into his posters is by focus: He moves in on the subject and in so doing seems to move it up and towards us. For instance, there is nothing happening in Win a Good Harvest (78), but the close-up "shot" of the girl allows us to feel that we've just seen her hoist the basket of grain; thus, we can "hear" the fisherman who sounds the alarm with his conch shell (105) because of such bold design.

Another criticism—like the others, no doubt a "western" criticism—is that too many posters are simply "cute." Look at poster 64, for instance. "That's too much" was my immediate reaction. And yet, in a society in which the soldier is an integral part of the community's everyday life, the poster makes a clear and direct statement. To us, who have almost no peacetime contact with our own military, it is indeed "a bit much." Likewise there is too much happiness in this collection; optimism is one thing, but an exaggerated always-on-camera smile becomes dull and induces cynicism, not to mention disbelief. The woman tractor-mechanic with wrench in hand (79): Is she always that happy in her grimey work or did she just stop long enough to say "cheese" to the artist with palette as she might to the visitor with camera? And the woman, high up on the telephone pole in the midst of a raging typhoon (74): Doesn't she realize that not even the Little Red Book will save her from pneumonia and, therefore, why is she smiling? And so it goes. Part of this may be an attitude on the part of westerners, faced with their own dissafection and the stultifying effect of their own assembly-line work, reacting in disbelief and possibly in jealousy when faced with the prospect that the most arduous and menial job could be so satisfying to others. To me, disbelief is the stronger reaction.

Another interesting aspect of these posters is that they show—in the posters themselves—the very central role played by the poster as a method of communication. In much of the West the poster as a viable, commercial marketing tool is in decline, but here in China, it is very much alive and well, selling dogma rather than deodorant, but selling effectively nonetheless. But, again, it is the fact of the prominence of the poster in the daily life of the Chinese shown in the posters themselves which is most unusual to us. The placing of posters on the hoardings is featured in over a dozen works in the collection and, most fascinating is the fact that even when one "takes up arms," (see, for instance, 66 and 101), the weapon is the posterist's brush: Is this a new society's variant of turning-the-swords-into-plowshares?

What it all comes down to is that a poster's job is to communicate a message, clearly and directly, to its intended audience. Since the vast majority of these were intended for internal consumption, a proper judgment of their effectiveness requires that we place ourselves in the shoes of the man-in-the-street of China today. And this orientation is quite difficult for us.

Finally, it should be mentioned that, unlike collecting many other types of original posters, gathering a large and varied set of current posters from China is a relatively easy and inexpensive hobby. Professor Fraser has suggested some of the ways to go about it. Through China publication offices in all major Western cities, one can purchase almost all the posters shown in this collection for anywhere from 50¢ to $5.00. So collecting 1970's posters from The People's Republic of China can be lots of fun, and their relatively small and uniform size (about 80% are 21 by 30 inches, or 53 by 77 cm) makes them easier to store and display than the larger-format posters from other countries. It should provide the collector with as much pleasure as gathering stamps or postcards from foreign countries; to see them in profusion and "in the flesh" is a visual delight.

Notes to the Posters:

In the notes provided by Professor Fraser which follow, the poster number corresponds to the page number. The title of the poster is given, followed by its size, with width preceding height. Size is to nearest half-inch and to nearest full centimeter. The dimensions of the entire printed sheet of poster are given and, likewise, it is the entire printed sheet that is reproduced here, not, as in the case of many books from China today, the image area only, with margins and text cropped out. This is followed by credit for the artist, where known, the name of the publisher, name of printer, and name of distributor. An Index number serves as the publisher's reference and the various printings, where indicated on the face of the poster, are given, as are the quantities printed and the price. It should be noted that many of these posters have had more printings than that indicated here, but the information provided is a translation of the facts which appeared on the poster photographed for this book.

—Jack Rennert
Editor, The Poster Art Library

13. PORTABLE BOOK SHELF. 21 x 30 in / 53 x 77 cm. By Chen Tsia-kang. Kansu People's Publishing House; Soo Chow Printing Press; Kansu Hsin Hwa Book Distributor. Index No. 8096-338. Price: 0.14 yuan.

The literary level of Chinese children today is high compared with their parents and grandparents. Reading is encouraged everywhere. Books are produced inexpensively and are widely distributed so that children have easy and ready access to them. Books even come to children, and the poster illustrates the popularity of the traveling mini-library which arrives by bicycle.

14. DON'T LET IT BLOW DOWN. 21 x 30 in / 53 x 77 cm. By Chew Ke-ping and Wu She-hu. Shanghai People's Publishing House; Shanghai No. 1 Printing Press; Shanghai Hsin Hwa Book Distributor. Index No. 8171-661. 1st Printing June 1973: 20,000. 2nd Printing July 1973: 1,000,000. Price: 0.11 yuan.

Community service, mutual support and even sacrifice are the themes involving moral values identified for children in this poster. Emulation techniques and individual exemplars are much in vogue to explain the canons of "good, right and proper behavior" for a Chinese child. The daily press, journals for juveniles, school textbooks and colored posters for general distribution continually stress the values of personal sacrifice for the common good and the slogan 'serve the people' is to be translated into a variety of deeds which should automatically flow from necessity. The boy and girl cooperate in fastening a young tree to its retaining pole in a windstorm. The primary level school children make a sacrifice by giving up their bookstrap to bind and save the tree.

15. NEW COMPETITORS. 21 x 30 in / 53 x 77 cm. By Kao Er-Yi, Cheong Wen-long, Tong Chiao-ming, Liang Ping-po. People's Fine Arts Publishing House; Peking Printing Press; Peking Hswin Hwa Book Distributor. Index No. 8027-6083. 1st Printing September 1975: 1,550,000. Price: 0.14 yuan.

"Friendship First and Competition Second" is the slogan emphasized at all sporting events in China. This sentiment is expressed on a "Sports Day" where the "Children's Relay Race" is a main feature and is proclaimed on the red banner over the judges' stand.

16. THE STORY OF TONG TSUNG-JUI. 21 x 30 in / 53 x 77 cm. By Lee Hui-foon and Chen Ting-chuong. People's Fine Arts Publishing House; People's Fine Arts Printing Press; Peking Hsin Hwa Bookshop Distributor. Index No. 8027-6065. 1st Printing June 1975; 500,000. 2nd Printing: 1,930,000. Price: 0.14 yuan.

The boy is declaiming the virtues of a youthful hero who is held up for boys and girls to emulate. The use of popular exemplars is a favorite topic for children's activities and is particularly encouraged in the schools.

17. LETTER TO LITTLE FRIENDS IN TAIWAN. 21 x 30 in / 53 x 77 cm. By Sie Chong-ing and Lin Ing-kan. Liaoning People's Fine Arts Publishing House; Chen Young No. 3 Printing Press; Liaoning Hsin Hwa Book Distributor. 1st Printing January 1975: 200,000. 2nd Printing September 1975: 530,000. Price: 0.11 yuan.

"Taiwan—always remembered, never forgotten" is an oft-proclaimed slogan. It is almost thirty years since Taiwan was 'lost' as an integral political part of China and the population, both adults and children, is reminded of "the island beyond the straits." In film, song and dance, children are told of their "missed cousins" in Taiwan, and the poster shown here stresses the need for continual remembrance as a letter is penned by the members of the Kong Ming Primary School and addressed to "Little Friends in Taiwan."

18. EXPRESS WITH WORDS. 30.5 x 21 in / 77 x 53 cm. By Au Yong and Yang Chih-kwang. Shanghai Book Publishing House; Shanghai City No. 2 Printing Press; Shanghai Hsin Hwa Book Distributor. Index No. 8172-289. First Printing, April 1977. Price: 0.30 yuan.

The traditional style painting shows a young Mao Tse-tung, some fifty years ago, as the nascent scholar, writer and teacher. The portrayal of Mao emphasizes his skills as a writer and theoretician with the journal *Political Weekly* shown on his left. This is one of the last available posters featuring Mao Tse-tung and was published in 1977. It was completed at the time of his death when Mao was engaged in writing and in adding to many of his earlier works.

19. RELATIONSHIP BETWEEN A TEACHER AND PUPILS IS AS CLOSE AS A FAMILY. 30 x 21 in / 77 x 53 cm. By Na Siu-ming, and Che Ing-jin. Tienching People's Fine Arts Publishing House; Tienching People's Printing Press; Tienching Hsin Hwa Book Distributor. Index No. 8073-20229. 1st Printing August 1975. Price: 0.14 yuan.

Mao Tse-tung said he wished to be remembered primarily as a teacher of his people, and this poster poignantly symbolizes this desire. The scene depicts Mao as a young man in rural south central China teaching children in a bamboo grove. In the background can be seen a village school called The Lenin Primary School, the newspaper is titled *Red China,* and the boy is holding an exercise book.

20. MODERN REVOLUTIONARY DANCE. 21 x 30 in / 53 x 77 cm. Shanghai People's Publishing House. Index No. 8-3-205. 1st Printing January 1971.

The "Red Detachment of Women" is one of the most popular of modern Chinese revolutionary ballet shows, and for nearly a decade it has received enthusiastic recognition both in China and abroad. The story illustrates the fortunes of a young woman, subjected to harsh treatment, who is forced to flee her family and eventually joins a band of women guerilla fighters. (The title of this dance is "Flushing Out the Tigers from the Caves"—after the arrest of Lo Tsu and Tuan Tin, Wu Ching Hwa springs out from hiding.)

21. MODEL COMMUNIST YOUTH MEMBER.—Wu Ye-tao. 21 x 26 in / 53 x 65 cm. By Chinese People's Liberation Army & Navy Art Workers Collection (Oil Painting). People's Fine Arts Publishing House. Index No. 8027-5402. 1st Printing Peking July 1971. Price: 0.12 yuan.

The poster extols the bravery of a naval pilot who rescued a friend from electrocution. The citation reads "When his comrade touched a live electric wire Navy Pilot Wu Ye-tao without hesitation pulled the wire away to save his comrade's life." The Central Military Committee commended Comrade Wu Ye-tao's action and conferred on him the title of "Model Communist Youth Member".

22. LONG LIVE THE PROLETARIAT. LEARN HARD FOR REVOLUTION. 30 x 21 in / 77 x 53 cm. By China People's Liberation Army, Air Force Political Department. People's Fine Arts Publishing House. Index No. 8027-5409. 1st Printing March 1971. Price: 0.16 yuan.

The poster commemorates the hundredth anniversary of the Paris Commune, established in 1871, after the defeat of France in the Franco-Prussian War. The Paris Commune was established as the revolutionary product of the siege and blockade of Paris by the Prussians. Lenin recognized the epoch-making nature of the Commune and his quotation appears in the top right side of the poster—"The Paris Commune showed that only the working class has experience for ruling. Force should be used to overthrow the oppressors." The worker is holding a copy of "Selections from Chairman Mao's Works" and the woman's arm band identifies her as a "Red Guard".

23. REVOLUTIONARY FRIENDSHIPS ARE DEEPER THAN THE OCEAN. 30 x 21 in / 77 x 53 cm. By Kok Hong-wu, Shanghai Tractor Factory. Shanghai People's Publishing House; Shanghai City No. 2 Printing Press. Shanghai Hsin Hwa Book Distributor. Index No. 8171-1331. 1st Printing August 1975. Price: 0.11 yuan.

Internationalism and the association of China with third-world nations, especially those of Africa, is the theme of this poster. Chinese development aid provided to African countries is symbolically represented by the group of African visitors, guests of the "Shanghai Tractor Manufacturing Factory". The tractor bears the trademark "Shanghai" and represents Chinese mechanical products exported throughout the world.

24. LONG LIVE THE UNITED PEOPLE OF THE WORLD. 42 x 21.5 in / 106 x 52 cm. By Chen Seng-wha. Shanghai People's Publishing House; Shanghai City No. 1 Printing Press; Shanghai Hsin Hwa Book Distributor. Index No. 8171-642. 1st Printing April 1973: 35,000 Price: 0.21 yuan.

Solidarity of the working people with revolution throughout the world is the obvious and exuberant theme of this poster. The central figure, as a symbolic leader of the revolutionary world, is a Chinese worker armed as a militiaman. His immediate comrades in arms to the left represent Korea, Vietnam, Cambodia and the Arab world, and to the right Albania, Japan and the African nations.

25. MODERN REVOLUTIONARY DANCE: RED DETACHMENT OF WOMEN. 33.5 x 21 in / 85 x 53 cm. Shanghai People's Publishing House. Index No. 8.31208. 1st Printing January 1971. Price: 0.10 yuan.

The "Red Detachment of Women" is recognized as one of the most popular modern ballets. The caption reads, "Train hard to develop skills for destroying the enemy. The Red Flag flies under the trees. Chinese peasants' and workers' Red Detachment of Women is officially formed. Graceful but strong, armed with rifles, the women soldiers are in high spirits to liberate countless suffering people and train hard to kill the enemy".

Premier Chou En-Lai, in 1963, is credited with recommending to the Peking Central Opera and Ballet Theatre that a contemporary ballet be produced. Early in 1964, members of the troupe visited Hainan Island, the locale for the original film, "Red Detachment of Women". In October 1964, the ballet was produced in Peking and received the mark of approval from Chairman Mao Tse-tung.

26. HARVEST SONGS AND DANCES. 21 x 30 in / 53 x 77 cm. Liaoning People's Publishing House; Sin Yang City Revolutionary Printing Press; Liaoning Hsin Hwa Book Distributor. Index No. 8090-362. 1st Printing August 1973: 200,000. Price: 0.11 yuan.

The end of summer and the gathering of the harvest is celebrated traditionally throughout China in song and dance. This beautiful poster, with shades of pink and red in dominance, portrays one of the minority peoples in northeast China celebrating the harvest. The group are Koreans, a minority which numbers some two million in China, who are found in the regions bordering on Korea. The men, women and children, for the most part, are dressed in Korean traditional costume, and the three central figures are performing a harvest drum dance. Traditional instruments include tambourines, reed instruments and bass drums, all accompanied by a modern accordion.

27. EARLY SPRING IN SOUTH CHINA. 21 x 30 in / 53 x 77 cm. Shanghai Fine Arts Publishing House; Shanghai No. 5 Printing Press; Shanghai Hsin Hwa Book Distributor. Index No. 8172-20. 1st Printing: 20,500. 2nd Printing: October 1973: 1,501,000.

The traditional style painting beautifully illustrates the ancient skill of rice cultivation integrated with the latest low-level technology of planting rice. The use of human labor combined with small machine-powered sleds or surface boats is a recent advance in rice cultivation. In the absence of difficult hillside terracing, the sleds, packed with rice seedlings, can easily traverse the large open rice fields. The combination of a graceful spreading willow tree and the electric power transmission poles and lines symbolizes the integration of natural features with modern technology.

28. NURSING. 30 x 21 in / 77 x 53 cm. By Liu Shi-wun. Ling Hsia People's Publishing House; Tien Shui Hsin Hwa Printing Press. Ling Hsia Hsin Hwa Book Distributor. Index No. 8157-212. 1st Printing February 1973. Price: 0.16 yuan.

This domestic scene reflects the many rural themes which insightful artists can capture through observing the multitude of everyday tasks of the villager. The flock of lambs is being fed from cow-horn flasks filled with milk, originally transported in the portable milk container shown at right.

29. TACHAI. 30 x 21 in / 77 x 53 cm. By Chang Yi-ching. Shanghai People's Publishing House; Shanghai City No. 5 Printing Press; Shanghai Hsin Hwa Book Distributors. Index No. 8171-1287. 1st Printing May 1975. 3rd Printing October 1975. Price: 0.11 yuan.

The name "Tachai" symbolizes the drive to "develop, improve and mechanize Chinese agriculture." Two decades before, Tachai, a village in the Taihang Mountains of Hsiyang County, Shansi, was poor, backward and unproductive. Through intensive collective efforts on the part of many individuals, the village received recognition for its bootstrap improvement. Tachai then became a symbol for self-reliance and self-sufficiency, and a slogan used throughout China today is "In Agriculture Learn from Tachai." Countless visitors are taken to Tachai to see at first hand what "self-help" means to a village which was once depressed and unproductive. The panorama, shown here in almost photographic style and detail, depicts Tachai in the Spring.

30. SPRING CULTIVATION. 30 x 21 in / 77 x 53 cm. By Li Feng-lan, Committee Member Kuangming Commune, Seehan village detachment. Shanghai People's Publishing House; Shanghai Cheong Hwa Printing Press; Shanghai Hsin Hwa Book Distributor. Index No. 8171-895. 1st Printing June 1974: 870,000. 3rd Printing January 1975: 1,170,000. Price: 0.11 yuan.

This painting is one of the most popular coming from the celebrated "Huhsien County Peasant Art Exhibition". It depicts a group of peasants in a semicircle hoeing and weeding in the cold of the early morning mist. Other farm workers are seen in the background spraying the young winter wheat while graceful swallows flit in between the workers crouched over their work. The artist, Li Feng-lan, a member of the Kuangming Commune, Huhsien County, Kuan-chung Region, has received widespread recognition for her paintings. In her own words, she describes how she approached her task of painting "Spring Cultivation": "So while I worked I started to observe carefully the people working around me, and during rest breaks I made sketches of them. It was on this basis that I started, amended and finally created 'Spring Cultivation'. It contains 16 persons, each of whom I had previously sketched. The middle-aged woman in the blue jacket in front is based on sketches of the women's team leader in our brigade. I started the painting in 1972 and from then till it was finished I kept collecting opinions and made many changes. The painting, exhibited in Peking last year (1973), was the fourth version. In it the portrayal of the people had improved somewhat."

31. STORM WARNING: PREPARE FOR SHELTER. 30 x 21 in / 77 x 53 cm. By Yin So-tsu, Peking Art Institute. Peking People's Fine Arts Publishing House; Peking City Hsin Hwa Book Distributor. Index No. 8071-162. Price: 0.14 yuan.

The flocks of sheep of the Mongolian herders represent their principal collective wealth and livelihood. Progress represented by the collectivization of the herds and the introduction of new techniques of livestock breeding is still dependent very much on the individual skills of the mounted shepherds. The roles of shepherd and mounted militia are interchangeable, and this is expressed by the weapons the shepherds carry, and by the fact they are accompanied by regular army cavalry. The title "Storm Warning" also has an alternative or double meaning, and reflects the concern for border security on the four-thousand mile frontier shared with a northern neighbor, the Soviet Union.

32. NA DA-NU FESTIVAL 30 x 21 in / 77 x 53 cm. By Pei Yi. Liaoning People's Publishing House; Pan Shi Printing Press; Liaoning Hsin Hwa Book Distributor. Index No. 8090-364. 1st Printing August 1973: 500,000. Price: 0.11 yuan.

The spring festival and meetings of various counties or family tribes of Mongols is the occasion for a variety of festivities including numerous horse racing events and exhibition of horsemanship. The banners depicted in this painting represent various nomadic families who have come together for the festival. The typical Mongol portable dwelling of woven wool panels, the yurt, is seen in the foreground.

33. GRASSLAND'S GREAT WALL. 30 x 21 in / 53 x 77 cm. By Chung Kwang-tsi, Heilungkiang People's Publishing House Collection. People's Fine Arts Publishing House. Index No. 8027-5729. 1st Printing Peking October 1973. Price: 0.11 yuan.

The Great Wall was designed many centuries ago to repel the invaders who wished to plunder or conquer China. The ancestors of the Mongols, portrayed in this poster, were amongst those who invaded China and for whom the wall was intended as a barrier. Today the mobile Mongol horsemen in the pasture lands are viewed as the equivalent of the Great Wall, providing the border with a protective screen against would-be invaders from the north. Mounted militia, both men and women, are viewing the scores of their target shooting from horseback. The flag identifies them as "Army Detachment Members."

34. LEARN FROM THE SPIRIT OF YENAN. 42 x 30 in / 106 x 77 cm. By Kok Yew-tong, Kwangchu Brigade. People's Fine Arts Publishing House. Index No. 8027-5742. 1st Printing Tienching, July 1973. Price: 0.22 yuan.

The spirit of Yenan teaches self-sufficiency and self-reliance. Thirty years ago the Communist armies were based in the Yenan area, and today their stories of sacrifice and comradeship are reconted for army recruits to follow. The soldier is engaged in "making and mending", an occupational undertaking of every soldier, while his comrades in the background are involved in harvesting with the people.

35. COASTLINE DEFENSE. 30 x 21 in / 77 x 53 cm. By Lin Tsing-yee. Liaoning People's Publishing House; Chen Yong Hsin Hwa Printing Press; Liaoning Hsin Hwa Book Distributor. Index No. 8090-552. 1st Printing June 1975: 300,000. 2nd Printing September 1975: 530,000. Price: 0.11 yuan.

The women's coastal militia unit is being instructed in "Enemy Warship Identification", as noted in the title on the illustrated charts, describing the "No.3 BKI Gun Boat" and the "MP2 Landing Craft". Naval instructors and coastal artillery are likewise portrayed in the poster as integral to the theme of coastal defense.

36. IMPROVE BATTLE ALERTNESS: TRAIN WELL IN TECHNIQUES TO DESTROY THE ENEMY. 21 x 30 in / 53 x 77 cm. By Liu Chong-yi, Kwangchou Regiment Art Collection. People's Fine Arts Publishing House. Index No. 8027-5744. 1st Printing Peking July 1973. Price: 0.11 yuan.

Military preparedness and the development of battle skills are the principal themes of this poster. The work is the product of a soldier with the Kwangchou Regiment. It represents an increasingly popular battle art style which has had much encouragement in the art exhibitions initiated by military units in recent years.

37. LEARN FROM LEI FENG. 21 x 30 in / 53 x 77 cm. By Ho Yu-tsu. Shanghai People's Publishing House; Shanghai City No. 2 Printing Press; Shanghai Hsin Hwa Book Distributor. Index No. 8171-625. 1st Printing July 1973: 400,000. 3rd Printing August 1973: 1,000,000. Price: 0.22 yuan.

Lei Feng is considered not only a modern day folk hero of children, but also a model for soldiers to emulate. His life as an army truck driver, while not spectacular, was ultimately worthy of attention and commendation after his death by Chairman Mao. Soldiers are encouraged to spend their spare time studying political works and integrating their activities with local communities, especially with the schools. There are four panels in this poster, two of which are illustrated in this collection. The left-hand one bears the inscription "Individualism is to be treated the way Autumn Wind treats the falling leaves—swept away." The right-hand panel indicates "The Enemy is to be treated the way Winter treats us—cool and cruel." The titles on the books read "Selections from Chairman Mao Tse-tung's Writings" and on the window "Learn Well from Mao Tse-tung's Works." (See also 61).

38. AFTER SCHOOL. 15 x 21 in / 38 x 53 cm. By Wu Pang-seng. People's Fine Arts Publishing House. Index No. 8027-5678 (4). 1st Printing Peking March 1, 1973. Price: 0.07 yuan.

"There are also just as important things to be learned outside of school" suggested Chairman Mao, and afterschool activities including physical education and sports are arranged for young people. This poster shows a physical education instructor from the Army conducting an after-school tug-of-war utilizing a practice dummy hand-grenade as the division marker.

39. A NEWCOMER TO THE MINE. 15 x 21 in / 38 x 53 cm. By Young Tsi-kwang. Kwangtung People's Publishing House; Kwangtung Hsin Hwa Printing Press; Kwangtung Hsin Hwa Book Distributor. Index No. 8111-1107. 1st Printing June 1973: 20,000. 2nd Printing August 1973: 100,000. Price: 0.16 yuan.

The traditional style painting depicts a young woman about to enter the elevator and descend into the mine. The integration of men and women in the work force, with many tasks being interchangeable, has given women encouragement to enter fields more habitually reserved for men. This painting has received nationwide acclaim, and this young woman miner is also depicted on a postage stamp set which illustrates the active role of women in the contemporary work force of China.

40. OUTDOOR CLASS. 30 x 21 in / 77 x 53 cm. By Tsao Ye-tien. Liaoning People's Publishing House; Liaoning Fine Arts Printing Press; Liaoning Hsin Hwa Book Distributor. Index No. 8090-548. 1st Printing June 1975: 500,000. Price: 0.11 yuan.

There are many things outside the confines of the formal classroom which should be taught. Learning to integrate theory and practice is the theme of this colorful poster. The outdoor class shows an experienced peasant in the commune's apple orchards supervising the teacher as she uses concrete examples in explaining arithmetic. The children are armed with abacuses, China's own traditional individual calculator. Boxes show that the apples are for export abroad and are appropriately labelled "Product of China".

41. THE REVOLUTION WILL CONTINUE FROM GENERATION TO GENERATION. 30 x 21 in / 77 x 53 cm. By Hunan People's Publishing House; Hunan Hsin Hwa No. 1 Printing Press; Hunan Hswin Hwa Book Distributor. Index No. 8109-978. 1st Printing June 1975. Price: 0.11 yuan.

China abounds in a variety of museums both small and large and catering to the tastes of adults as well as children. Many museums focus on the historical and contemporary class struggle of the peasants and their landlords or the life of serfs and slaves under ancient China's rulers. The future generation, the children, are depicted in this poster as eager students of the peasants who are instructing them in the realities of their harsh past. The museum contains memorabilia of peasant uprisings, oppressive landlord contracts and the documents of class struggle. The children are shown visiting the Museum of Peasant History and are being instructed in the oppression suffered by their parents and grandparents. The wall plaques provide an appropriate quotation from Chairman Mao's writings: "The peasants' revolt in the village disturbs the sweet dreams of all those rich landlords . . .".

42. CULTURAL TEAM VISITS A FISHING VILLAGE. 30 x 21 in / 77 x 53 cm. By Lee Yi. Liaoning People's Publishing House; Chen Yong 7212 Printing Press; Liaoning Hsin Hwa Book Distributor. 1st Printing August 1975: 100,000. Price: 0.2 yuan.

The role that itinerant troupes of entertainers play in China is a traditional one, and this poster depicts a culture group arriving at a fishing village. Propaganda and education integrated into plays, songs and dances, are the common stock of the traveling teams who are responsible for visiting isolated communities and keeping them abreast of social and political events. The scene shows the cultural troupe complete with its musical instruments and entertainment props. The villagers provide a warm welcome for the visitors in anticipation of the concerts which will follow.

43. WELL DRILLING EQUIPMENT BUILT BY AN COMMUNE. 30 x 21 in / 77 x 53 cm. By Chung Ho-yung and Chua Tzu. Sun Tong People's Publishing Collection. People's Arts Publishing House. Index No. 8027-5730. 1st Printing Peking June 1973.

Water, its finding, control and distribution, are central to the lives of Chinese farmers. Flood and surplus often go hand in hand with scarcity and elusiveness. In many parts of China, storage dams and irrigation channels provide the principal means of irrigation. The concept of deep well digging is likewise a familiar one. Mechanical drilling, using portable rigs and utilizing locally made machine equipment, reflects a low-level technological breakthrough. Power drilling emphasizes both the up-to-date nature of agricultural techniques and the self-reliant and localized nature of the product. The scene shows the successful operation of a small portable mechanical drill and the ensuing flow of water confirming the faith placed in the local commune's ability to manufacture equipment which can function properly.

44. LITTLE ELECTRICIANS. 30 x 21 in / 77 x 53 cm. By Yung Pau-sing and Yee Chin-lei. Liaoning People's Publishing House; Liaoning Fine Arts Printing Press; Liaoning Hsin Hwa Book Distributor. Index No. 8090-343. 1st Printing June 1973: 100,000. 2nd Printing August 1973: 300,000.

Childrens' meeting halls and clubhouses for youth activities are found throughout China. An extensive range of afterschool activities, hobbies, and sports are normally a feature of these establishments. Among the hobbies are usually found a wireless and communication club encouraging the building of such items as wireless sets.

45. CHILDREN FOLLOWING IN THE FOOTSTEPS OF TACHAI. 30 x 21 in / 77 x 53 cm. By Lu Chung-kwi, Peking Teachers' College, Member of Workers', Peasants' and Soldiers' Revolutionary Art Section. Peking People's Publishing House; Peking Hsin Hwa Book Distributor. Index No. R8071-174. 1st Printing November 1975. Price: 0.14 yuan.

The name of the rural community of Tachai in Shansi County is often regarded as synonymous with the concept of self-help and perseverance in the face of adversity (See also 29). Children are encouraged in their combined work and study programs to remember the message and lessons of Tachai. The children in the poster are identified as coming from "The Yenan Primary School" and in building the terraces for their "School Farm" are reminded of Tachai by the slogans on the distant hillsides: "In Agriculture Learn from Tachai."

46. A FARMING VILLAGE IS OPEN COUNTRY. 30 x 21 in / 77 x 53 cm. By Kao Chuan. Peking People's Fine Arts Publishing House. Index No. 8027-5798. 1st Printing 1 November 1973. Price: 0.11 yuan.

The city's newcomer is welcomed to the agricultural commune. Youngsters graduating from high school are expected to spend at least two years on a farm doing manual work. The woman tractor driver, as signified by her overalls, is a member of the Chen Sin Commune. The slogan cut into the mountainside again proclaims "In Agriculture Learn from Tachai".

47. MILITARY TRAINING IS FOR REVOLUTION—SPINNING AND WEAVING ARE FOR THE PEOPLE. 30 x 21 in / 77 x 53 cm. By Yung Son-Chin, Shanghai Weaving Work Committee Art Group. Shanghai Peoples Publishing House; Shanghai Fine Arts Printing Press; Shanghai Hsin Hwa Book Distributor. Index No. 8171-597. 1st Printing March 1973: 330,000. 4th Printing August 1973; 600,000.

The poster is the product of a factory

worker from a Shanghai cotton mill who depicts fellow workers engaged in friendly competition between teams striving to excel. The slogan reads "Encourage Hard Work, Struggle to the Top, Advance the Building of Socialism". Heading on the blackboard reads "Group Work Production Schedule," and the inscription on the women's aprons indicates "Shanghai Weaving Mill".

48. IF THE ENEMY COMES FROM THAT DIRECTION! 15 x 21 in / 38 x 53 cm. People's Fine Arts Publishing House; Peking No. 2 Printing Press; Peking Hsin Hwa Book Distributor. Index No. 8027-5828. 1st Printing March 1974: 277,000. Price: 0.07 yuan.

This traditional Chinese style painting shows an experienced peasant militiaman explaining to the children the role they may play in guerilla war to harass an invader. Military preparedness on the part of China's people, whether adults, students or young children, is a theme of great popularity for poster art. Here, village youngsters are placing mines in a road to foil the enemy. The awareness of danger from potential invaders is a perennial topic and China's population has been conditioned over many years to rely on local resources in order to repel those who "could have designs on Chinese territory."

49. DON'T DEPEND ON THE GODS. 21 x 30 in / 53 x 77 cm. By Sian Mechanical Works Art Group. Shanghai People's Publishing House; Shanghai Chun Hwa Printing Press; Shanghai Hsin Hwa Book Distributor. Index No. 8171-1217. 1st Printing April 1975. 2nd Printing July 1975. Price: 0.11 yuan.

The caption on the painting is self-explanatory, extolling as it does the mastery of man over nature, and the self-sufficient nature of China's peasantry in building its own destiny without recourse to religion or fear of superstition. The style is unusual but clearly evocative of peasant paintings now much the vogue throughout many parts of China. It is the product of a Mechinal Factory Art Group from Sian, the old west central Chinese capital. The inscriptions on the walls of the buildings seen in the picture are "The People's Will is Greater than God's" (bottom left) and "Long Live Chairman Mao" (top right).

50. WE CHALLENGE THE SUN AND MOON TO CHANGE THE NEW WORLD. 30 x 21 in / 77 x 53 cm. By Peking City Agricultural and Mechanical Department; Irrigation Workers' Fine Arts Group. People's Fine Arts Publishing House. Index No. 8027-5750. 1st Printing August 1973. Price: 0.11 yuan.

The Yellow River, running from west to east through north-central China has been for thousands of years the scourge of that country. The harnessing of the river's flow and power for agriculture has long been the goal of successive Chinese rulers but it is only during the last two decades that more significant results have been achieved and now it has been shown that indeed man could control the river. The slogan erected by the workers digging the control levee banks states "Determined to Tame the Yellow River."

51. PEASANTS AND WORKERS GREETING THE NEW YEAR. 30 x 21 in / 77 x 53 cm. People's Fine Arts Publishing House; Printed in the People's Republic of China; Peking China International Book Distributor. Index No. 86-643.

New Year or Spring Festival Prints are popular in China; they signify the turning point in winter and the approach of spring. The tractor group is on its way to a celebration in a snowscape typical of the severe weather that dominates nearly half of northern China during the winter months. The bright equipment and banners contrast with the starkness of the snow, contributing to an exuberant picture for the festival holiday.

52. EXPERIMENTAL FARM. 30 x 21 in / 77 x53 cm. People's Fine Arts Publishing House; Printed in the People's Republic of China; Peking China International Book Distributor. Index No. 86-645.

This striking poster, utilizing the sea, fishermen and marine seafood technology as its theme, is illustrative of the scientific approach and research orientation that China is taking in many aspects of food production. Marine biology, fish farming and seaweed cultivation go hand in hand to increase the quantity and quality of the sea harvest so necessary for China's livelihood and nutritional levels. The picture shows forms of seaweed and kelp being scientifically checked. The glass float has a sign identifying "Experiment No. 2".

53. COMMUNE FISH POND. 30 x 21 in / 77 x 53 cm. By Tung Cheng yi. People's Fine Arts Publishing House; Peking No. 2 Printing Press; Peking Hsin Hwa Book Distributor. Index No. 8027-5808. 1st Printing March 1973: 1,370,000. 2nd Printing March 1973: 1,870,000. Price: 0.11 yuan.

The cultivation of fish in fish ponds is a traditional Chinese rural peasant activity but its growth during the past decade has been phenomenal in terms of productivity, the result of applied research and extensive experimentation. Fish is a staple diet item of not only coastal villagers but is relied upon as a supplement by many inland rural communities who use China's extensive river systems to create fish ponds for their supplies.

This painting, one of the Huhsien Peasant Agricultural Paintings, exemplifies the bountiful and spectacular nature of the crop to be gathered by net in the fish ponds of the commune. It is one of the most spectacular and brilliant of the peasant painting genre to appear in the collection and by vivid colors and fine design, with the swirling of people and net and leaping of fish, cleverly catches the seething mass of golden and yellow carp as they are trapped in the net.

54. THE BRIGADE'S DUCKS. 30 x 21 in / 77 x 53 cm. By Li Chen-hua. People's Fine Arts Publishing House; Printed in the People's Republic of China; China International Book Distributor. Index No. 86-625.

This poster and the following one illustrate some of the finest work shown at the Huhsien County Peasant Agricultural Paintings Exhibition in Shensi Province. There is an almost lyrical, impressionistic feeling to both these fine works and they have been immensely popular not only in China but throughout the world.

55. BRIGADE CHICKEN FARM. 30 x 21 in / 77 x 53 cm. By Ma Ya-li. People's Fine Arts Publishing House; Printed in the People's Republic of China; China International Book Distributor. Index No. 86-626.

This is another fine example of the Exhibition of the Huhsien County Peasant Agricultural Paintings of Shensi Province. As with many other posters in this collection and mass-produced in China today, there is no date given, but its first printing was probably in 1973. Whether its domestic intent (where it was published without three-language captions) was to encourage poultry raising or its international intent is to show a dynamic, grass-roots agricultural movement, its effect, first and foremost, is to impart great aesthetic pleasure.

56. TODAY'S "FOOLISH OLD MEN" CREATE NEW SCENES. 21 x 30 in / 53 x 77 cm. By Cheng Min-sheng and Chang Lin. People's Fine Arts Publishing House; China International Book Distributor.

This is also included in the exhibition of the Huhsien County Peasant Agricultural Art. An old Chinese folk story relates the tale of an old man who tried to move mountains by taking stones away, one by one. His neighbors ridiculted him and conferred on him the title of "Foolish old man who tried to move mountains." However, the last laught was on the neighbors and their descendants because he persisted, with the help of his children and, in turn, their children, until eventually his dream came true. The posters—we show only the first two of a sequential set of four panels—demonstrate the start made to "foolishly remove stones" and the end result of a soundly constructed irrigation project.

57. BRIGHT SPRING—THE PRODUCTS OF SKILLED HANDS. 21 x 30 in / 53 x 77 cm. By NaTsu-min. Tienching People's Fine Arts Publishing House; Tienching People's Fine Arts Printing Press; Tienching Hsin Hwa Book Distributor. Index No. 8073-20163. 1st Printing June 1973. Price 0.11 yuan.

This work may also be included in the genre of spring festival posters and depicts the highly intricate work of the carpet and rug makers. China has long been famous for the production of serviceable and beautiful carpets. It therefore comes as no surprise to note that the Tienching People's Fine Arts Publishing House has produced this poster, for Tienching is one of the major centers of the rugmaking industry in China today. The designs range from flamboyantly spectacular, as portrayed in the peacock tapestry hanging from the wall, to the more standard flower designs which the workers are in the process of finishing.

58. CHANGING DAY BÝ DAY. 30 x 21 in / 77 x 53 cm. By Ta Lien Ling Tong Mechanical Workshop Art Group. People's Fine Arts Publishing House, Peking. Index No. 8027-5598. 1st Printing October 1972. Price: 0.07 yuan.

The shipyard working at full production around the clock best exemplifies the desire on China's part to produce and be self-sufficient in major industrial items which were once entirely imported. The ship-building industry is a spectacular example. This print is the product of Ta Lien, a famous northeastern coastal seaport and shipbuilding center which vies with Shanghai for first place in the industry. Themes associated with naval construction have long been popular for the posterist, either originally executed in gouache or, as in this case, in wood block.

59. CHILDHOOD. 21 x 15 in / 53 x 38 cm. By My Sing-tong. People's Fine Arts Publishing House. Index No. 8027-5676. 1st Printing January 1973. Price: 0.07 yuan.

The portrayal of the degradation which occurred in former times and the contrast afforded with contemporary or new China are favorite topics for the artist. Many museums and exhibitions have dioramas and life-like displays depicting the harsh and oppressive life before the establishment of the People's Republic in 1949. The illustration shows children, some in minorities' dress, viewing the exhibitions which reminds them that the childhood of their parents often involved tears and bitterness.

60. YOUNG EAGLE SPREADING HER WINGS. 15 x 21 in / 38 x 53 cm. People's Fine Arts Publishing House; People's Fine Arts Printing Press; Hsin Hwa Book Distributor. Index No. 8027-5827. 1st Printing March 1974: 595,000. Price: 0.07 yuan.

This traditional style painting portrays the grace and beauty of a young girl as she proceeds through an exercise under the watchful eye of her proud teacher. The martial skills involving sword exercises are of traditional importance in China, but in recent years they have had an extraordinary popular revival and are a feature of the physical culture program of many schools.

61. LEARN FROM COMRADE LEI FENG. 21 x 30 in / 53 x 77 cm. By Fang Lei-chi. Shantung People's Arts Publishing House; Shantung Hsin Hwa Book Distributors. Index No. 8099-182. Price: 0.13 yuan.

The schoolgirl is performing her tasks of public service by sweeping up and by exhorting her fellow students to follow the example of Lei Feng. He is regarded as a modern day folk hero whose fine example of "service to the people" is extolled for emulation by Chinese boys and girls. Posters depicting the life and activities of Lei Feng are to be found in schools throughout China. Lei Feng was a squad leader of a People's Liberation Army Transportation Company who died at his post on August 15, 1962, aged 22—"His life, though short and ordinary, was great". A laudatory commendation by Mao Tse-tung in March 1963 brought national attention to the virtues displayed so humbly by an ordinary army truck-driver. Mao himself coined the phrase which is the title of this poster. (See also poster 37.)

62. LEARN WELL AND IMPROVE EVERY DAY. 30 x 21 in / 77 x 53 cm. By Chang Chou City Workers', Peasants' and Soldiers' Fine Arts Group. Shanghai People's Publishing House; Shanghai City No. 9 Printing Press; Shanghai Hsin Hwa Book Distributor. Index No. 8171-469. 1st Printing December 1972: 850,000. 3rd Printing August 1973: 1,050,000. Price: 0.11 yuan.

This is a poster for children extolling Chairman Mao's teaching that "Students should not only study books but should also study from the workers, peasants and soldiers" (top center panel). The girl's badge signifies that she is a member of the Little Red Guard and she is shown with a "Primary School Book" on her desk. The blackboard has "World Revolution" written on it. The four panels which comprise the poster depict children's activities both within and without the normal confines of the school.

63. BUDDING TOWARDS THE SUN. 30 x 21 in / 77 x 53 cm. By Low Siew-kwi, Tang Chu-er, Chen Fong, Liu So-tang and Fung Chwin. Peking People's Publishing House; Peking Hsin Hwa Book Distributor. Index No. R 8071-107. Price: 0.14 yuan.

West Lake in Peking, with Coal Hill in the background, is the locale for this poster depicting the Red Guard activities of children in their "palaces" or clubhouses. Many summer activities are portrayed in meticulous detail. The slogan on the clubhouse wall states "Learn Well, Improve Daily". The pavillion at top left announces the celebration of June 1, Children's Day. Floats in the water accompanying the children read "Struggle Ahead in the Stormy Winds and Big Waves" and "Firstly Don't Fear Hardship, Secondly Don't Fear Death".

64. ARMY AND PEOPLE ARE ONE FAMILY. 21 x 30 in / 53 x 77 cm. By Hang Kwang-chou. People's Fine Arts Publishing House. Index No. 8027-5612. 1st Printing September 1973. Price: 0.11 yuan.

The slogan inscribed on the window states "Support the Army, Love the People". The young boy, holding his toy rifle, is sitting on the soldier's pack, while receiving a haircut from a "servant of the people".

65. SUN AND RAIN NURTURES NEW BUDS. 21 x 30 in / 53 x 77 cm. By Chang Tong-ping. Shanghai People's Publishing House; Shanghai Fine Arts Printing Press; Shanghai Hsin Hwa Book Distributor. Index No. 8171-605. 1st Printing July 1973: 500,000. 2nd Printing August 1973: 700,000. Price: 0.11 yuan.

The cutaway doll's-house style poster illustrates many of the activities undertaken in a typical Children's Palace. These buildings, for children from eight to fifteen years of age, are designed for a variety of afterschool activities ranging from sports to arts and from science to handicrafts. The activities depicted include physical education, music, songs, dances, drama, drawing, puppeteering, acupuncture, science and astronomy. The slogan on the main building reads "Long Live Chairman Mao" and those on the door pillars "Improve Daily" and "Learn Better". The three squads of children in the bottom right hand corner are: in Group 1, "Learn from the Workers"; Group 2, "Learn from the Peasants"; and Group 3, "Learn from the Army". In the extreme bottom right hand corner is a sign which identifies the "Herbal Garden."

66. FOLLOW TONG TSU'S FIGHTING SPIRIT. 30 x 21 in / 77 x 53 cm. By Hsia Wun-chen. Kwangtung People's Publishing House; Kwangtung Hsin Hwa Printing Press; Kwangtung Hsin Hwa Book Distributor. Index No. 8111-1441. 1st Printing July 1973. Price: 0.14 yuan.

The children are reminded of the youthful hero who, armed with brush and ink, made his own posters and wrote his own words. Those who follow are likewise expected to write their own "big character" and "little character" posters, and the children, guided by their teenage leader, are ready to do battle with brush and ink, ladders, glue, paper and pail. The heading on the poster wall reads "March Forward and Criticize Lin Piao and Confucius." The artist of this poster is a student at a Middle (secondary) School.

67. RED GARDEN. 30 x 21 in / 77 x 53 cm. By Pai Yi-ru. People's Fine Arts Publishing House; Peking No. 2 Printing Press; Hsin Hwa Book Distributor. Index No. 8027-6117. 1st Printing June 1975; 500,000. Price: 0.14 yuan.

The criticism of Lin Piao and Confucius is the continuing theme of many posters and this is appropriately recorded on the "Notice Board." The Little Red Guard has her hand on the "Educational Revolution 1974", the vertical poster at left states "Popularize Revolutionary Spirit" and the poster being completed on the ground reads "Fighting for the Cultural Revolution".

68. TRAIN HEADING FOR SHAO SHAN. 30 x 21 in / 77 x 53 cm. By Chai Ni-chin. Peking People's Publishing House; Peking Hsin Hwa Book Distributor. Index No. 8071-105. 1st Printing August 1973. Price: 0.14 yuan.

In a kindergarten setting, this poster illustrates one of the collective games played by young children, namely "Train" which is destined for Shaoshan, Chairman Mao's birthplace, now a highly revered shrine visited annually by countless Chinese and foreign visitors. The children in the "train" are dressed in the colorful costumes representing several of the various minority peoples of China including Uighers, Koreans, and Mongolians. Three of the children are dressed to represent the classless trinity embodied by workers, peasants and soldiers. To complete the symbolic representation of society, there is an equal number of boys and girls in the kindergarten group!

69. GRASSLAND PRIMARY SCHOOL. 30 x 21 in / 53 x 77 cm. By Ma Chin-yang. Liaoning People's Publishing House; People's Fine Arts Printing Press. Index No. 8027-5234. 1st Printing July 1973. Price: 0.11 yuan.

The painting features Mongolian chilren learning their lessons in an "outdoor classroom". The traditional house or yurt is in the background with a tractor nearby, symbolizing the modernization of some aspects of nomadic life. Sheep and horses are also in the picture and represent the major sources of their livelihood.

70. BE A GOOD SERVANT FOR THE PEOPLE. 30 x 21 in / 77 x 53 cm. By Chen Chun-chan. Tienching People's Arts Publishing House; Tienching People's Printing Press; Tienching Hsin Hwa Book Distributor. Index No. 8073-20244. 1st Printing November 1975. Price: 0.11 yuan.

The children are learning practical arithmetic problem solving during an excursion to the market. Armed with abacuses and notebooks, they are being introduced also to the concept of serving the people which is the slogan printed on the apron of the vegetable seller. And the vegetables, which frame the teacher and students in the center, steal our attention: They are voluptuous in their quality and color.

71. FAMILY PLANNING FOR REVOLUTION. 30 x 21 in / 77 x 53 cm. By Hsiang Yang. Shanghai People's Publishing House; Shanghai City Printing Press; Shanghai Hsin Hwa Book Distributor. Index No. 8171-852. 1st Printing March 1974: 530,000. Price: 0.11 yuan.

The concept of family planning is widespread in China and is a major preoccupation of the government in its quest to limit population growth to manageable proportions. China's population is in the vicinity of 870 million today and may grow to over 1 billion by the year 2000. Accordingly, the continuing campaign to limit family size and space the birth of children is coupled to the improvement of child and maternal care. The book is titled "Family Planning Propaganda Handbook". On the apron is stenciled the slogan "Grasp the Revolution, Increase Production". The bottle is labeled "Oral Contraception Tablets". The slogans on the top and bottom of the poster read "Learn from Marxist Theory and Chairman Mao's Thought for the Benefit of Future Generations and Education; Improve Women's and Children's Health; Grasp the Revolution; Encourage Production; Encourage Work; Encourage Struggle; Benefit the Nation and National Prosperity".

72. ACUPUNCTURE. 21 x 30 in / 53 x 77 cm. By Shau Hwa. People's Fine Arts Publishing House. Index No. 8027-5724 (2). 1st Printing September 1973. Price: 0.11 yuan.

Medical personnel of The People's Liberation Army are shown at work with minority peoples in Mongolia. The doctor is being instructed in the use of acupuncture, the soldier explaining the method from an acupuncture diagram of the ear.

73. PICKING HERBS. 21 x 30 in / 53 x 77 cm. By Liu Chi-ho. Liaoning People's Publishing House; Anh Sun Hsin Hwa Printing Press; Liaoning City Hsin Hwa Book Distributor. Index No. 8090-365. 1st Printing August 1973: 500,000. 2nd Printing October 1973: 1,710,000. Price: 0.11

The gathering of herbs for both medicinal and culinary reasons is traditional, but recently there has been a revival of herbal medicine and the use of herbs in a variety of health related fields. This has encouraged the cultivation and gathering of the multitudinous species of useful herbs located throughout China. The girl's Red Cross satchel suggests both the medical reasons for the excursion into the hillside and the hazards sometimes associated with gathering herbs.

74. I AM A SEA SWALLOW. 15 x 21 in / 38 x 53 cm. By Fan Cha-ling. People's Fine Arts Publishing House. Index No. 8027-5595 (4). 1st Printing February 1973. Price: 0.07 yuan.

The military are responsible for maintaining communications throughout China. The woman, a member of a signals and communication unit, is repairing telephone lines after a coastal typhoon. Engaged in a hazardous operation, she is depicted with leg clamp irons, rigger's belt and telephone testing equipment. This poster was produced from an original oil painting.

75. BRAVERY AND GRACE GO TOGETHER. 21 x 30 in / 53 x 77 cm. By Liu Fan-ying, Pei Kai-sing, and Ma Huh-Fanshun Art School. Peking People's Publishing House; Peking Hsin Hwa Book Distributor. Index No. 8071-159. 1st Printing November 1975. Price: 0.14 yuan.

The women's militia unit is practicing winter tactics in the snow. The theme of military preparedness may be seen in conjunction with border security in the northern regions of China bordering on the Soviet Union. The women are practicing an attack on a bunker or tank position using the attachable satchel-pack explosive charges.

76. REVOLUTIONARY TEACHERS AND STUDENTS ARE THE SAME AS THE COMRADES FIGHTING AT THE FRONTLINE. 30 x 21 in / 77 x 53 cm. By Fang Yen-chung. People's Fine Arts Publishing House; Peking Printing Press; Hsin Hwa Book Distributors. Index No. 8027-5940. 1st Printing September 1974: 450,000.

The poster suggests teachers and students should be engaged together in political activities in the campaign to criticize Lin Piao and Confucius (as noted in the poster slogans on the left). The wall slogan proclaims "Education Must Serve the Need of the Proletariat". The student, with the help of her teacher, is preparing a poster presumably based on material supplied by the theoretical magazine, Red Flag, seen on the table.

77. FRUITFUL MORNING. 31 x 20 in / 77 x 53 cm. By Feng Chun-yi and Heu Soo-kuang. Liaoning People's Publishing House; Sen Yan 7212 Printing Press; Liaoning Hsin Hwa Book Distributor. Index No. 8090-372. 1st Printing August 1973: 100,000. 2nd Printing September 1973: 480,000. Price: 0.11 yuan.

The colorful and cheerful early morning scene shows the apple pickers on their way to work by bicycle. All the women are mounted and the bicycles, privately owned, may reflect an advanced level of individual prosperity. It is also interesting to note that although all women wear slacks, only one (second from left) is riding a "woman's model" bicycle.

78. WIN A GOOD HARVEST—INCREASE GRAIN PRODUCTION. 42 x 30 in / 106 x 77 cm. Shanghai People's Publishing House; Shanghai City No. 2 Printing Press. Index No. 8171-630. 1st Printing April 1973: 20,000. Price: 0.22 yuan.

A good grain harvest ensures that the problem of food shortages for the coming year has been lessened. China has to fight drought and floods, as well as inclement weather to produce the necessary crops to feed her people. The poster has an exuberant mood, signifying expectations for a good harvest. The red and gold slogan on the basket proclaims "Communes are Good" and the slogan on the grain stacks (right) indicates "Fight Wars and Fight Famine for the People".

79. STRUGGLE TO INCREASE THE MECHANIZATION OF AGRICULTURE. 42 x 30 in / 106 x 77 cm. By Peking City Central Committee No. 76. People's Fine Arts Publishing House. Index No. 8027-5487. 1st Printing December 5, 1971. Price: 0.22 yuan.

The mechanization of agriculture is an important goal in increasing food production throughout China. While some areas may be unsuitable for the widespread adaptation of mechanical equipment, many others are able to increase production through mechanization and more scientific farming. The tractor operator-mechanic has inscribed on her overalls "Agricultural Mechanical Workshop" and the poster in the background of the maintenance yard again proclaims "Fight Wars and Fight Famines for the People".

80. STUDYING. 15 x 21 in / 38 x 53 cm. By Chin Chow-tsui and Lin Yong. People's Fine Arts Publishing House; Peking Printer 2nd Printing House; Peking Hsin Hwa Book Distributor. Index No. 8027-5826. 1st Printing March 1974: 230,000. Price: 0.07 yuan.

The farming peasant and factory worker is encouraged to learn and study in his spare time. Advancement, in order to serve the people better, requires continual study for better ideological understanding or technical improvement. The agricultural note in the picture is present with the grain, ears of corn, and bunch of peppers hanging from the ceiling. Current newspapers and copies of the journal Red Flag, as well as various textbooks, make up the necessary study materials.

81. OLD PARTY SECRETARY. 21 x 30 in / 53 x 77 cm. By Liu-Chih-teh. Shanghai People's Publishing House; Shanghai City No. 1 Printing Press; Shanghai Hsin Hwa Book Distributor. Index No. 8171-890. 1st Printing June 1974: 1,040,000. 2nd Printing January 1975: 1,340,000. Price: 0.11 yuan.

This poster has been widely acclaimed for its sensitivity and style in representing the maturity and wise leadership of experienced party members. The artist, who is Party Secretary of the Chin Tu Commune, Chin Sun Brigade, is paying respect to older comrades with whom he has worked.

This was one of the posters in the Huh-sien County Peasant Painting Exhibition and a Chinese appraisal of it notes: "Among the most popular of the Huh-sien paintings is 'Old Party Secretary.' The artist . . . moves viewers by his concrete delineation of a vital person. He does not resort to posters or symbols detached from typical situations or typical characters. The elderly secretary's weather-beaten face, his grizzled hair, big rough hands and plain clothing all show that he continues to work with his hands, that his heart has never left the people, that he is a man steeled through many trials, yet warm and approachable. . . It is not by chance that Liu Chih-teh could paint such a portrait. Himself a brigade party secretary, he is thoroughly familiar with the life and thinking of such cadres. And as a preliminary step he made sketches of many Party Secretaries." We are left to assume that the best one was selected for reproduction here.

82. HARMONIZE A NEW SONG. 30 x 21 in / 77 x 53 cm. People's Fine Arts Publishing House. Index No. 86-637. Peking International Book Distributor.

Since urban youngsters and older citizens alike are required to participate in rural experiment in "living, learning and laboring," posters play a role in preparing them for some of the benefits of bucolic life. The painting notes the aesthetic and cultural aspect of village life for young people as they learn to sing a new song entitled, "Be Good Farmers for the Revolution." The characters on the overall signify membership in the Tong Tiang Commune, the book is entitled "New Battleground

Songs" and the slogan stenciled on the hat reads "Put Your Heart Into Farming."

83. SERVE WORKERS, PEASANTS AND SOLDIERS; JOIN WORKERS, PEASANTS AND SOLDIERS. 42 x 30 in / 106 x 77 cm. Peking People's Fine Arts Publishing House; Guozi Shudian, China Publication Centre. Index No. 86 CEFG-573.

The leading groups in today's Chinese society are workers, peasants and soldiers. The girl with the red lantern symbolizes youth, and the older man with the peasant headscarf represents the experienced party member providing leadership to these three social elements.

84. DEPEND ON YOUR OWN STRENGTH; FIGHT HARD, ACCELERATE THE BUILDING OF SOCIALISM. 30 x 42 in / 77 x 106 cm. By Shanghai Shipyard Propaganda Arts Group. Shanghai People's Publishing House. Index No. 8171-577. 1st Printing January 1973: 20,000. Price: 0.22 yuan.

Naval construction workers on the evening shift in one of Shanghai's several large shipyards is the theme of this poster. China's determination to be self-sufficient ultimately in a variety of fields includes the essential coastal shipping and international trade. Hence the ship-building industry is one of the priority enterprises whose production capacity is being increased.

85. TALL RISING CHIMNEYS CHANGE THE SKYLINE. 21 x 30 in / 53 x 77 cm. By Kwei Toe-chong. Hopei People's Publishing House; Hopei People's Printing Press; Hopei Hsin Hwa Book Distributor. Index No. 8086-405. 1st Printing October 1974: 80,000. Price: 0.14 yuan.

The poster puts into context the old and the new, the young and the aged. The young women and the old men are looking together at the rising products of China's newly developing technology. The old man with his cart and horse is of the generation representing old China, and the young women boilermakers and welders personify the coming generation of new China's workers. The poster also illustrates the responsible role played by women in the construction industry and their capability to tackle all kinds of tasks utilizing their newly-taught technical skills.

86. BEFORE GOING ON SHIFT DUTY. 21 x 30 in / 53 x 77 cm. By Tsao Shitsing. Hopei People's Publishing House; Hopei People's Fine Arts Printing Press; Hopei Hsin Hwa Book Distributor. Index No. 8086-525. 1st Printing October 1975: 330,000. Price: 0.14 yuan.

The guard, a "Duty Officer" according to her armband, is testing her batteries and flashlight before going on duty. On the table, Lenin's work on "Nation and Revolution" is her current reading matter.

87. USING COLLECTIVE METHODS WE CAN MAKE BIGGER DISCOVERIES. 21 x 30 in / 53 x 77 cm. By Liu Siew-pin. Tienching People's Fine Arts Publishing House; Tienching Peoples Art Printing Press; Tienching Hsin Hwa Book Distributor. Index No. 8073-10132. 1st Printing May 1973. Price: 0.11 yuan.

The role of science and technology in improving the lot of the people is the theme of this poster. The woman scientist, a marine biologist, is encouraged by the slogans in the background—"Convert bad to good; Convert waste to use".

88. COMING TO A SECOND HOME. 21 x 30 in / 53 x 77 cm. By Yan Winkung and Chan Yu-ping. Shanghai Book Publishing House; Shanghai Cheong Hwa Printing Press; Shanghai Hsin Hwa Book Distributor. Index No. 8172-54. 1st Printing January 1974: 200,000. Price: 0.14 yuan.

The government encourages urban dwellers to migrate to the country to infuse new blood into agriculture and that, in fact, is the theme suggested by this poster. The older woman, appropriately dressed for severe winter conditions, accompanies a younger traveler taking a train to her "second home." During the last decade over one million graduates of Shanghai middle schools have been sent off to the countryside. "Going up to the mountains and down to the villages" has become a way of life.

89. PUT YOUR HEART INTO FARMING. 21 x 30 in / 53 x 77 cm. By Shi Tek-yen. People's Fine Art Publishing House. Index No. 8027-5732. 1st Printing Peking June 1973. Price: 0.11 yuan.

Nearly eighty per cent of China's people live in rural areas and virtually all of them must earn their living directly from some form of agriculture and animal husbandry. Migration to rural areas and the resettlement of virgin frontier lands by young people from the cities has been a regular pattern for China during much of the past two decades. In a desire to introduce Chinese urban youth to the concept of agricultural manual labor, millions of high school graduates have been sent down to the countryside to face life on the farm for the first time. This is a difficult period in their lives and they often need the guidance of the vereran farm workers. Hence the often-seen slogan, here shown on the girl's apron: "Put your Heart into Farming".

90. GIVING BIRTH: THE SUCCESS OF SKILLED HANDS. 21 x 30.5 in / 53 x 77 cm. By Liu Yang-whan. Lioaning People's Publishing House; Lioaning Fine Arts Printing Press; Lioaning Hsin Hwa Book Distributor. Index No. 8090-560. 1st Printing September 1975: 85,000. Price: 0.11 yuan.

A successful birth is indicated in the happy expressions on the part of the army nurse, barefoot doctor, and grandmother watching expectantly from the adjoining room. The medical equipment may also suggest a caesarean operation; abdominal retraction instruments and intravenous injection equipment indicate the extent of the operation. The locale is a room at home rather than a hospital, and on the wall is a commendation certificate of the kind often used in China to recognize long service.

91. SHANGHAI CITY EYE AND SKIN HOSPITAL. 21 x 30 in / 53 x 77 cm. By Cheng Yi-hao. Shanghai People's Publishing House; Shanghai City No. 1 Printing Press; Shanghai Hsin Hwa Book Distributor. Index No. 7171-12. 1st Printing February 1973: 380,000. 5th Printing January 1974: 445,000.

The concept of using eye exercises is traditional but only in the last few years has it come into more popular vogue. The Diagram for Eye Health Exercises reads: "(1) Close your eyes when doing the exercises and follow the timing of the records;)2) Keep you fingers clean and finger-nails short; (3) Massage the precise points gently until it feels somewhat tired. Do not apply too much pressure—it might harm the eyeballs: (4) Exercise regularly twice daily, once in the morning and once in the afternoon; (5) Maintain good eye hygiene."

It should be noted that this kind of instructional chart in poster form is seen throughout classrooms and clinics in China and they do not differ very much in design or purpose from the school posters in the West meant to impart instructions to students, such as Presidential Charts in the United States or Royal Succession Charts in England, and the like. Only one such example is included here because, for obvious reasons, they lack graphic appeal.

92. GO TO SCHOOL WITHOUT WORRYING ABOUT THE WIND AND RAIN. 30 x 21 in / 77 x 53 cm. By Liu Ne-hao. Shanghai People's Publishing House; Shanghai City No. 1 Printing Press; Shanghai Hsin Hwa Book Distributor. Index No. 7171-97. First Printing December 1973: 65,000. Second Printing October 1974: 235,000. Price: 0.16 yuan.

The poster encourages children not to fear the wind and rain but to come to school irrespective of the weather. Half a dozen children, armed with umbrellas or oilskins, wend their way along the street towards the "Red Star Primary School". The poster was first produced for the City's Primary School by the Shanghai City Middle School and Primary School Teaching Material Collection Group.

93. CHILDREN'S HEALTH EXAMINATION DAY. 30 x 21 in / 77 x 53 cm. By Chung Tsu-kun and Lee Chin. Hopei People's Publishing House; Hopei People's Fine Arts Printing Press; Hopei Hsin Hwa Book Distributor. Index No. 8086-502. 1st Printing October 1975: 320,000. Price: 0.11 yuan.

The poster highlights the role of the barefoot doctor and the village clinic in safeguarding children's health through regular medical examinations. The wall poster in the background exhorts "Proclaim Late Marriage and Birth Control", "Liberate Women Workers".

94. RESOLUTELY SUPPORT THE STRUGGLE OF THE AFRICAN PEOPLE AGAINST COLONIALISM AND RACIAL DISCRIMINATION. 30 x 21 in / 77 x 53 cm. Shanghai People's Publishing House; Guozi Shudian (International Bookshop Peking), Distributor. Index No. 86 CEF 574.

The revolutionary spirit of modern Africa is depicted in this dynamic and heroic monument. The original sculpture has been photographed and transposed to poster format for eventual worldwide distribution. The accompanying text is provided in English, French and German.

95. UNITE TOGETHER AND FIGHT FOR GREATER VICTORY. 30 x 21 in / 77 x 53 cm. By Kiang Nan-choon. Shanghai People's Publishing House; Shanghai City No. 2 Printing Press; Shanghai Hsin Hwa Book Distributor. Index No. 8171-738. 1st Printing September 1973: 4,000,000. Price: 0.11 yuan.

All the major nationalities and minority peoples have representation in this poster which highlights Mao Tse-tung's portrait hung outside the Great Hall of the People In Peking's Square of Heavenly Peace. The left panel reads "Long Live Our Great Leader Chairman Mao", and the right panel, "Long Live the Great Chinese Communist Party".

96. LEARN THE HEROIC SPIRIT AND FOLLOW THE HEROIC ROAD. 21 x 30 in / 53 x 77 cm. By Mung Yang-yi. Peking People's Fine Arts Publishing House; Peking People's Printing Press; Peking Hsin Hwa Book Distributor. Index No. 8027-6063. 1st Printing October 1975: 500,000. 2nd Printing October 1977: 680,000. Price: 0.11 yuan.

The group of women are on an excursion to visit a heroine's memorial. They are exchanging experiences as they undertake their pilgrimage to learn from an experienced cadre. The inscription on the hat reads "In Agriculture Learn from Tachai".

97. NEW YEAR IN YENAN. 21 x 30 in / 53 x 77 cm. Shen-si People's Fine Arts Publishing House. Index No. 8027-5609. 1st Printing August 1973. Price: 0.14 yuan.

Mao Tse-tung is surrounded by men, women, and children representing all segments of the community found at Yenan, the Chinese Communist base in the 1930's and 1940's. The poster includes boys and girls in winter festive clothing as well as a variety of soldiers and peasants. The children are holding decorated pink lamps with the slogan "Be Self-Sufficient, Use Your Own Resources".

98. FEBRUARY 7TH CELEBRATION—PEASANTS AND WORKERS UPRISING (1923-73). 30 x 21 in / 77 x 53 cm. By Chen Chow Railway Department. Hunan People's Publishing House. Index No. 8105-387. 1st Printing December 1972. Price: 0.14 yuan.

The poster shown here celebrates the 50th anniversary of an uprising and strike by workers on the Peking-Hankow Railway. The banner identifies the "Workers of the Peking-Hankow Railway Line." The hand-held small yellow poster at the left says "Down With Imperialism," and those on the right proclaim "Down with the Military Police." Across the bottom are the words of a revolutionary song commemorating the occasion: "Steel in the Military Police's Hands. Blood on the Workers' Necks. Necks can be broken, bones can be crushed, but the fighting spirit will not be destroyed. All Working People Unite Together."

99. MARCH FORWARD TO ACHIEVE GREAT PROLETARIAN CULTURAL REVOLUTION. 30 x 21 in / 77 x 53 cm. By Ho Yi-min, Teng Su, Ko Shang-yi, Chen Jian-ling, Hoo Konglui, Yuan Hao, Yang Lui-kui. People's Fine Arts Publishing House. Index No. 8027-5618. 1st Printing August 1973. Price: 0.14 yuan.

The Great Proletarian Cultural Revolution commencing in the mid 1960's saw immense political convulsions that disturbed China until the 1970's. The involvement of young people and the formation of the Red Guards as vanguard fighters for the Cultural Revolution, is strikingly portrayed in this poster. The scene in Tien An Men Square, (The Square of Heavenly Peace) was duplicated many times during the Cultural Revolution as millions of Red Guards as well as factory workers and commune peasants converged on the capital to greet and hear Chairman Mao Tse-tung. The poster at left proclaims "Long Live the Communist Party of China". The inscription on the flat at right is "Follow Chairman Mao's Long March". This poster is the result of a collective effort on the part of seven artists. It was published in 1973, by which time the major controversies of the Cultural Revolution had abated somewhat.

100. IRON BASTION—JOINT DEFENCE BY THE ARMY AND THE PEOPLE. 21 x 30 in / 53 x 77 cm. People's Fine Arts Publishing House, Peking; Distributed by China Publications Centre, Peking. Index No. 86 CEFG-569.

The protection of China's boundaries and its defense in depth depend on the involvement and alertness of its local militia units. The people's Liberation Army on frontier duty is responsible for the training and integration of militia units with regular army units. "Iron Bastion" is a symbolic painting and one of a genre which calls for the Chinese people to show eternal vigilance on the border areas.

101. WORKERS, PEASANTS AND SOLDIERS ARE THE MAIN FORCE TO CRITICIZE LIN PIAO AND CONFUCIUS. 30.5 x 41 in / 77 x 105 cm. By Lou Chia-pan. People's Fine Arts Publishing House; Peking Printing Press; Peking Hsin Hwa Book Distributor. Index No. 8027-5895. 1st Printing March 1974. Price: 0.22 yuan.

The familiar triumvirate of workers, peasants and the military dominates this powerful poster. The woman holds her speech in readiness while the soldier is armed with poster brush. The worker, holding "Selections from Chaiman Mao," is seen smashing a sign representing the old and the corrupt, personified once again by Lin Piao an Confucius.

Lin Piao's fate perhaps best symbolizes the quixotic, all-or-nothing policy of the Government. For many years a close associate of Mao, he became defense secretary when the Communist government was installed, and in 1966, during purges occasioned by the Cultural Revolution, he emerged as the Number 2 man in the hierarchy. Yet in 1972, only six years later, it was suddenly announced that Lin Piao died "in a plane crash" after attempting to seize power on behalf of the Soviet Union. The abortive coup and alleged flight by plane supposedly took place the year before (1971).

102. INCREASE ALERTNESS, STRENGTHEN MILITARY TRAINING. 21x30 in/53x77 cm. By Chiang Chong-Po, Lui Chiao-mun of Shanghai Electric Cable Factory. Shanghai People's Publishing House; Shanghai No. 1 Printing Press; Shanghai Hsin Hwa Book Distributor. Index No. 8171-987. 1st Printing September 1974. Price: 0.11 yuan.

Two workers of a Shanghai cable factory are responsible for this poster; it was first exhibited at a display of "Factory Worker Art" in Shanghai. The artists have used their own factory for the background and have successfully included several different aspects of militia training. Aircraft recognition, communication skills, fire drills, anti-aircraft and anti-tank drills, as well as small unit tactics, bayonet drills, and grenade throwing are all featured. The poster on the noticeboard reminds the factory militia to "Fight Wars and Fight Famines for the People."

103. TRAINING HARD TO KILL THE ENEMY. 21x30 in/53x77 cm. By Fu Kwang Tao. Tienching People's Fine Arts Publishing House; Tienching Hsin Hwa Book Distributor. Index No. 8073-10136. 1st Printing June 1973. Price: 0.11 yuan.

The machine gunner in action during night maneuvers represents the genre of posters which extols national military preparedness; they are frequently seen in China. It is a strikingly effective poster, implying aggressive movement and with a momentum of its own which gives life to the poster and, no doubt, assures death to this gunner's enemy.

104. EAGLES SPREADING THEIR WINGS. 30x21 in/77x53 cm. By Tong Sieng-ming. Hopei People's Publishing House; Hopei People's Fine Arts Printing Press; Hopei Hsin Hwa Book Distributor. Index No. 8086-475. 1st Printing October 1974: 970,000. 2nd Printing May 1975: 1,570,000. Price: 0.11 yuan.

Members of a Mongolian mounted militia unit are depicted undergoing target practice. Women are central to the poster's theme and their representation provides support for their enhanced recognition in society, especially within that of the Mongolian people.

105. WILLING TO COME WHEN CALLED. 30x21 in/77x53 cm. By Wu Ming. Tienching People's Fine Arts Publishing House; Tienching People's Printing Press; Tienching Hsin Hwa Book Distributor. Index No. 8073-10137. 1st Printing December 1973. Price: 0.11 yuan.

The alarm is sounded; it calls the coastal militia members to arms. This striking poster focuses on the conch sea shell as the alarm signal in the hands of an armed fisherman. In the background can be seen a fleet of small fishing boats responding to the call. The full title of the poster is: "Willing to Come when Called; Able to Fight when Here; Able to Sacrifice when Fighting."

106. LEARN FROM THE PEOPLE, FOR THE PEOPLE. 30x42 in/76x107 cm. By the Shanghai Militia Art Group. Shanghai People's Publishing House; Shanghai City No. 2 Printer; Shanghai Hsi Hwa Book Distributor. Index No. 8171-640. First Printing April 1973: 15,000. Price: 0.22 yuan.

"The people and the military are one family" is one of the mottos often stressed (as in poster 64, for instance). This scene illustrates the spirit of cooperation between soldiers and civilians, both of whom have been called out to sweep the streets clear of the winter snow. The slogan on the building reads "Long Live the Dictatorship of the Proletariat."

107. BELOVED PREMIER CHOU EN-LAI IS ALWAYS WITH US. 13.5 x 29 in / 35 x 73 cm. Peking People's Publishing House; Hsin Hwa Book Distributor. Index No. 8071-243. 1st Printing Peking, January 1977.

Chou En-lai became Premier in 1949 and held this position for 26 years until his death on January 8, 1976 in Peking; this poster is one of many issued a year later to commemorate his death. The widespread popularity of Chou has

been a feature of the intra-party struggles that have occurred in China after his death. His death and anniversary provoked demonstrations in many cities in China and gave testimony to the high place he holds in the hearts of the Chinese people.

108. WHOLE HEARTEDLY CRITICIZE THE GANG OF FOUR. 41 x 30.5 in / 105 x 77 cm. By Wong Yung-chuan, Shanghai Art Institute. Shanghai People's Publishing House; Shanhai City No. 1 Printing Press; Shanghai Hsin Hwa Book Distributor. Index No. 8171-1934. 1st Printing January 1977. Price: 0.28 yuan.

The Gang of Four gets told off by a militant older worker, joined in his resolve by the girl, probably a recent secondary school graduate, who is holding "Selections From Chairman Mao's Writings." The caption on the poster reads: "In Industry Learn from Taching; In Agriculture Learn from Tachai; Be Raised to a High Tide." The slogans on the tower note "Strongly criticize the Gang of Four" and "Be Independent and Be Your Own Master."

The Gang of Four chosen for such vituperation in this and other posters in this collection include Mao's widow, Chiang Ching, and three of her colleagues, Wang Hung-wen, Chan Chun-chiao, and Wen Yuan, who supposedly intended to usurp power after Mao's death in September 1976. They were stripped of all titles and party memberships, and denounced for an incredible variety of crimes against the people, the party, the economy and the government.

109. WATER SPORT CARNIVAL. 29.5 x 21 in / 75 x 53 cm. By Kang Ing-lian and Chang Hong-liu. Kwangtung People's Publishing House; Shing Kiang People's Printing Press; Kwangtung Hsin Hwa Book Distributor. Index No. 8111-1256. 1st Printing October 1974. Price: 0.14 yuan.

We witness here a waterborne tug-of-war between two teams of paddlers representing the people and the army. The scoreboard lists the competing teams in "The Military and People's Combined Water Sports." On the bridge is the slogan "The People's Communes are Good."

110. REVOLUTIONARY COMMITTEES ARE GOOD. 30 x 21 in / 77 x 53 cm. By Lin Kang-hwa, Chen Soo-chung, Chung Kuo-fang and Chang Wai-kung. People's Fine Arts Publishing House; Peking People's Printing Press; Peking Hsin Hwa Book Distributor. Index No. 8027-

6389. 1st Printing June 1976: 40,000. Price: 0.14 yuan.

The multicolored woodcut-style poster is the product of four artists; how the labor was divided we do not know. The banners held by the workers proclaim "The Establishment of Revolutionary Committees," and "Long Live Great Leader Chairman Mao."

111. A THOUSAND SONGS AND MILLION DANCES FOR THE COMMUNIST PARTY. 30 x 21 in / 77 x 53 cm. By Yin Chia-liang. Shanghai People's Publishing House; Shanghai Cheong Hwa Printing Press; Shanghai Hsin Hwa Book Distributor. Index No. 8171-1329. First printing December 1976. Price: 0.14 yuan.

The official recognition of Chairman Hua Kuo-feng as China's new leader is exemplified in this recent poster: Minority peoples are represented as paying respect and greetings to Hua as Chairman of the Communist Party. The pervading and continuing ideological influence of Mao Tse-tung may be noted by the soldiers symbolically holding a copy of Mao's works beside Hua's own picture.

112. SIX HUNDRED MILLION PEOPLE. 21x29 in/53x74 cm. By Song Hui-tun. Kwangtung People's Publishing House; Kwangtung Fine Arts Printing Press; Kwangtung Hsin Hwa Book Distributor. Index No. 811-1523. First printing June 1976. Price: 0.14 yuan.

The five panels illustrate with fine attention to detail many of the daily activities associated with the various Chinese nationalities, including Mongols, Thais, Uighers, Koreans and Tibetans. Reading from top to bottom, slogans and notices read: *1st Panel*—left, "Revolutionary Committee;" right-hand noticeboard, "Continually Criticize Lin Piao and Confucius;" the newspaper is the *People's Daily;* and the man is holding a poster which again says "Criticize Lin Piao and Confucius." *2nd Panel*—"In Industry Learn from Taching" and "In Agriculture Learn from Tachai." *3rd Panel*—"May 7 Cadre School" next to the blackboard; on it is written "Political Night School" and "Learn Well the Political Theory of the Proletariat;" at left, "University Physics Department, 1976." *4th Panel*—table tennis players hold a plaque: "Friendship First, Competition Second." *5th Panel*—on hat, "Defend the Frontier;" and on milk bucket, "Sooching Brigade."

The complete title of this poster is the title of a poem attributed to the late Chairman Mao: "Six Hundred Million People in This Beautiful Country, Everyone Should Work Hard to Build our Beautiful Motherland."

Author's Acknowledgments

I would like to acknowledge the interest and involvement of many persons who have contributed to the collection. In particular I would like to thank the cadre staff and all the workers of the Chang Chun Provincial Branch of the Hsin Hua Printing House, in Chang Chun, Kirin Province. It is a little over a year ago that I was privileged to spend some time in the grounds and works of the Printing House during a visit to North East China. It was of inestimable value to have them explain to me the overall organization of the factory of the departments concerned with poster and art production. I was shown the process starting from the design and art studio through to the color separation and printing works. I met with photographers, artists, layout specialists, color printers, and distribution workers. The factory employs some fourteen hundred workers of whom forty

percent are women; in addition, each month the factory provides work for nearly two hundred secondary students who come to undertake practical work from the various towns throughout Kirin Province. Many of the students have exhibited their own art work at the factory and some have been offered a chance to see their work chosen for nationwide distribution as posters published by this printing house.

There are innumerable Chinese workers who have kindly assisted in my quest for posters in various Chinese cities. Appreciation to them is also recorded for their many courtesies, particularly to the staff of New China News Agency, Guozi Shudian, and Foreign Languages Press all of whom were most helpful.

To Shaw Tan, a colleague, much appreciation is acknowledged for his painstaking efforts in

translating poster titles and the details of printing specifications concerning each poster; and to Kathryn and Lachlan Fraser and to Therese McNeil thanks go for their kind assistance in preparing the poster annotations and textual material. I would also like to thank my publisher, Jack Rennert, for his interest, patience, and persistence in seeing this collection compiled and published in its present form. His assistance and thoughtful suggestions have been integral to the final publication of this collection of poster art from the People's Republic of China, a country which uses the medium of poster to an extent hitherto unrealized in most countries.

—Stewert E. Fraser
Melbourne, Australia
November, 1977

流动书箱

不让它吹倒

新　　手

董存瑞的故事

信儿捎给台湾小朋友

激扬文字 邓澍 纸之合作

亲 切 的 关 怀

革命现代舞剧 **红色娘子军**

冲出虎狼窝

顽强得到胜利后的吴清华，摆脱走出魔掌下的威胁，急速奔向胜利。

模范共青团员胡业桃

海军航空兵某部导航连战士胡业桃，当战友触电的时候，毫不犹豫地拉过电线，用生命
保护了战友的安全。中共中央军委为表彰胡业桃同志，特授予"模范共青团员"的光荣称号。

革命友谊深如海

革命现代舞剧 红色娘子军

丰收歌舞

郑新丽 作

保育

春 锄助 (透门户县农民画展)

早已森严壁垒

那达慕盛会

草 原 长 城

想延安时代学延安精神

海防线上

提高路线觉悟 练好杀敌本领

（三）对待个人主义要象秋风扫落叶一样

（四）对待敌人要象严冬一样残酷无情

課 余 （中国画）

矿 山 新 兵

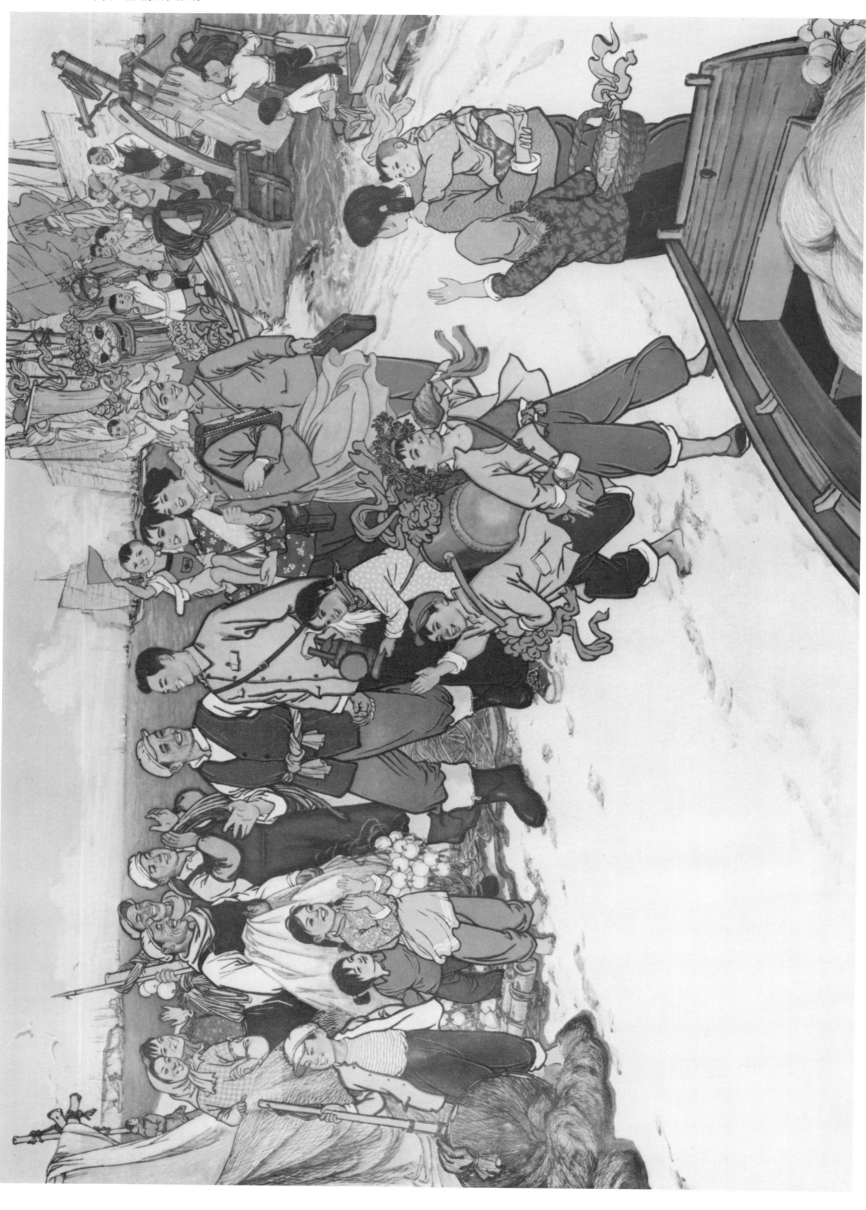

俺 社 创 造 了 打 井 机

「电工」小

从小就走大寨路

46

操作练兵为革命 纺纱织布为人民

如果敌人从那边来 (中国画)

不靠天

敢 教 日 月 换 新 天

工 农 一 家 喜 迎 春

中国国际书店发行
中国·北京
Printed in the People's Republic of China

武 验 田

Printed in the People's Republic of China

公 社 鱼 塘

THE BRIGADE'S DUCKS   LES CANARDS DE LA BRIGADE DE PRODUCTION   DIE ENTEN DER PRODUKTIONSBRIGADE

Printed in the People's Republic of China

54

BRIGADE CHICKEN FARM　　LE POULAILLER DE LA COMMUNE　　DIE HÜHNERFARM UNSERER PRODUKTIONSBRIGADE

中国国际书店发行
中国·北京

Printed in the People's Republic of China

当代愚公绘新图

（选自户县农民画展）

（一）

当代愚公绘新图

（选自户县农民画展）

（二）

巧 手 织 出 春 光 来

日　新　月　昇　（版画）

大连市苦老城厂企业美术编创组作　人人口美术出版社印刷出版（次印次111次印）

童　年　（油画）

雏 鹰 展 翅 （中国画）

向雷锋同志学习

XIANG　　LEIFENG　　TONGZHI　　XUEXI

毛主席语录

学生也是这样，以学为主，兼学别样，即不但学文，也要学工、学农、学军，也要批判资产阶级。

好好学习 天天向上

HAO HAO XUE XI TIAN TIAN XIANG SHANG

花 儿 朵 朵 向 阳 开

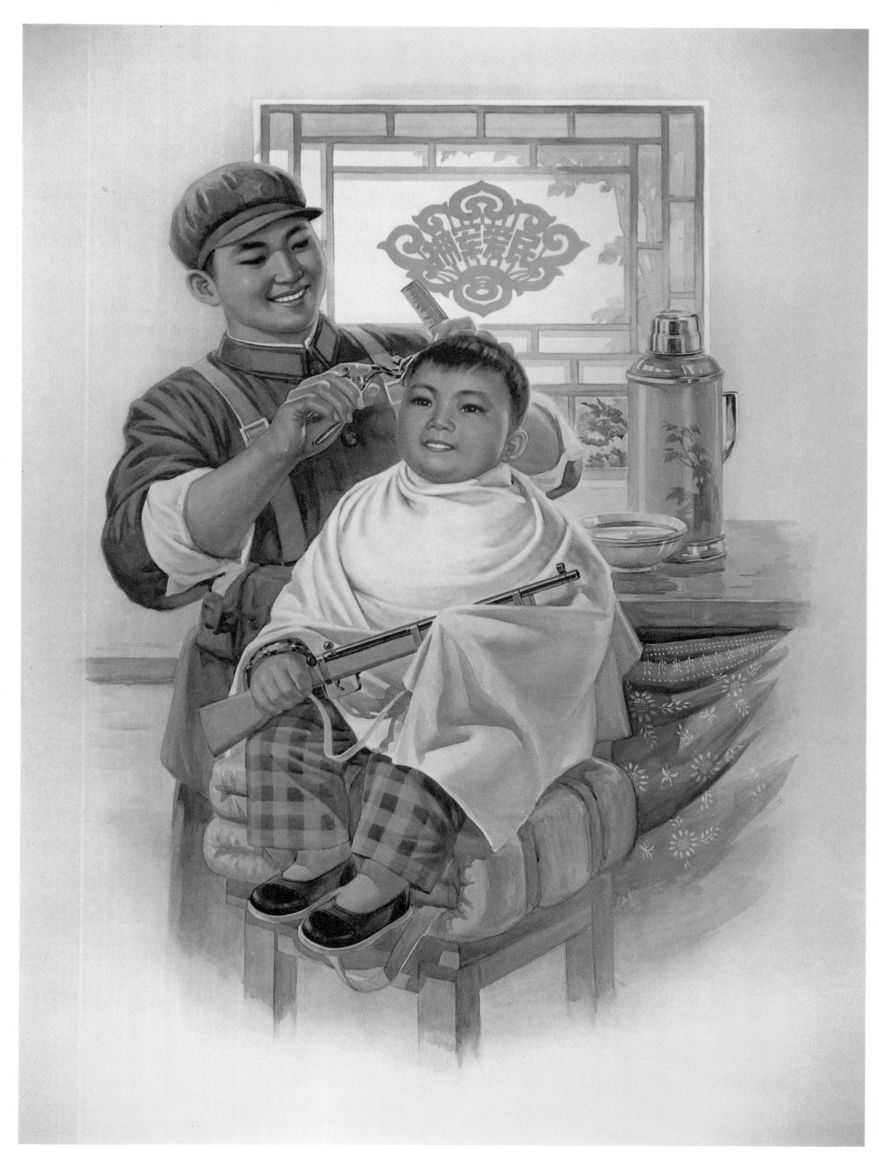

军 民 一 家 亲

阳光雨露育新苗

红 色 园 地

火车向着韶山跑

草原小景

当好人民勤务员

试　　　针

采药

"我 是 海 燕" （油画）

英姿飒爽

果 乡 的 早 晨

为加速实现农业机械化而奋斗

攻　读　(中国画)

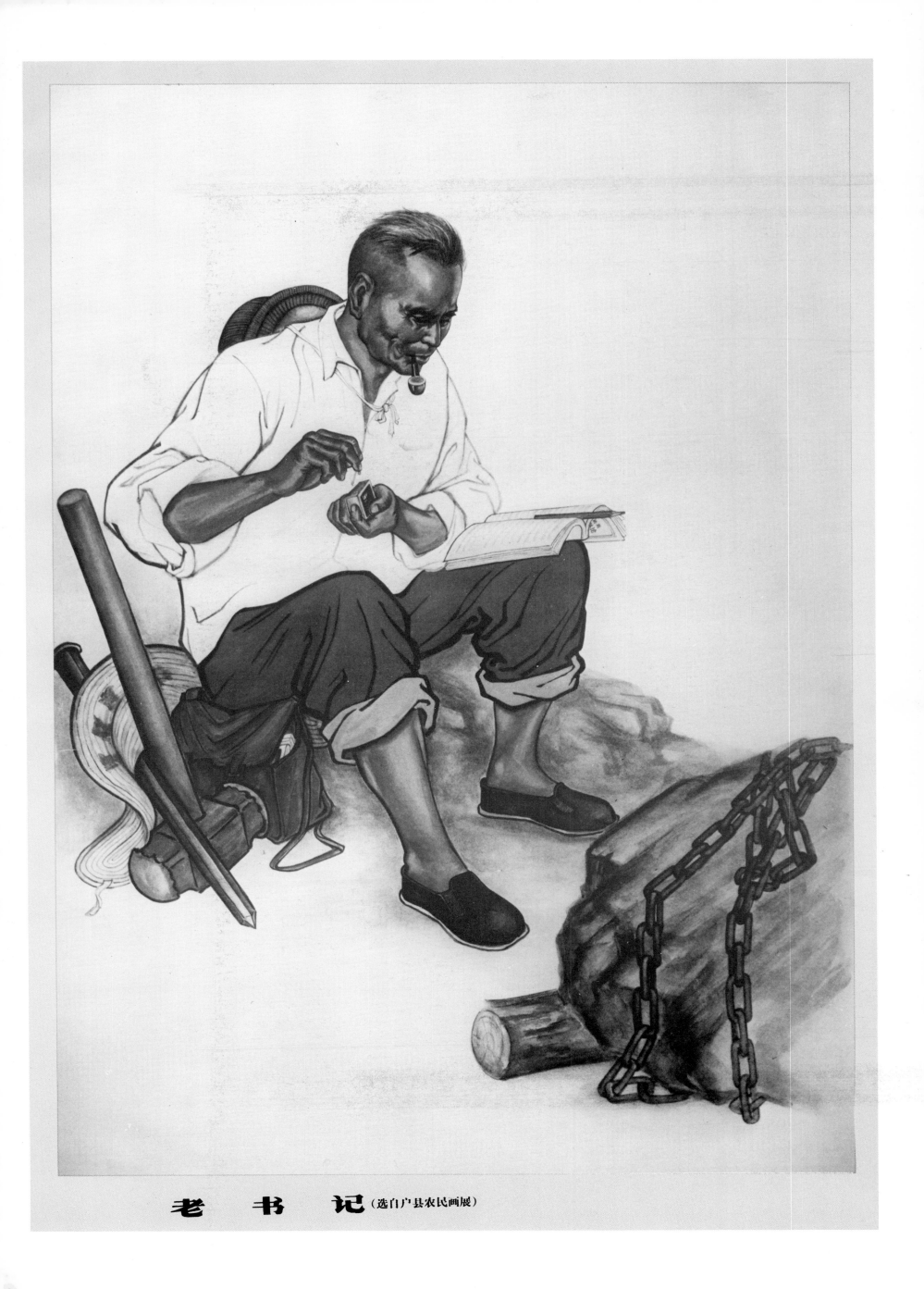

老书记 （选自户县农民画展）

猛 禽

为工农兵服务，同工农兵结合!

Serve the Workers, Peasants and Soldiers; Link Oneself
with the Workers, Peasants and Soldiers!

Servir les ouvriers, paysans et soldats, et
s'intégrer à eux!

Dient den Arbeitern, Bauern
verbindet euch mit ihnen!

自力更生 艰苦奋斗 加快社会主义建设

高炉层层起　太行日日新

换 岗 之 前

综合利用 大有文章可做

ZONG HE LI YONG DA YOU WEN ZHANG KE ZUO

来到第二个故乡

一九七三年青年节政惠允 张世年 合作

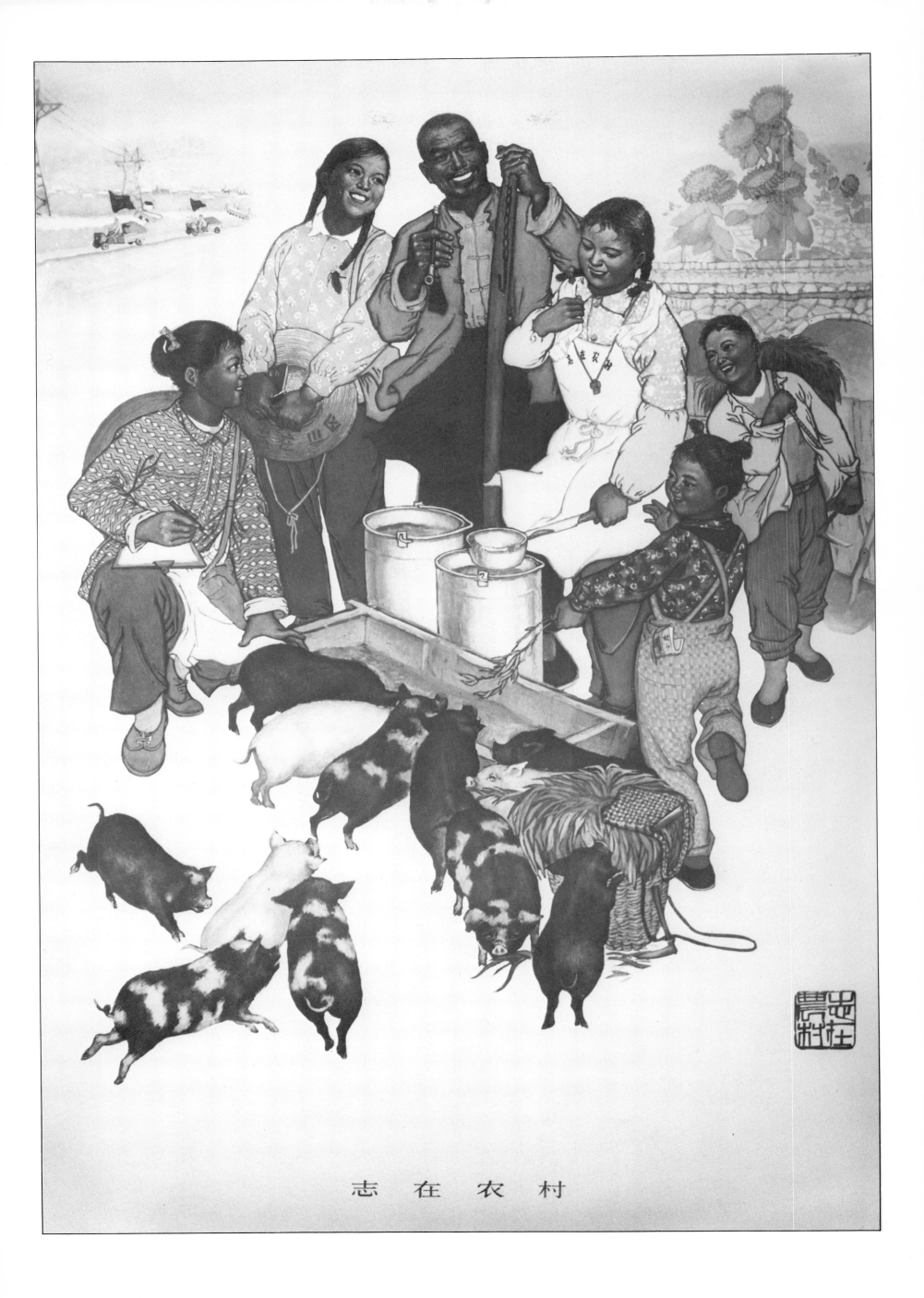

志 在 农 村

成功的手术

眼保健操图解

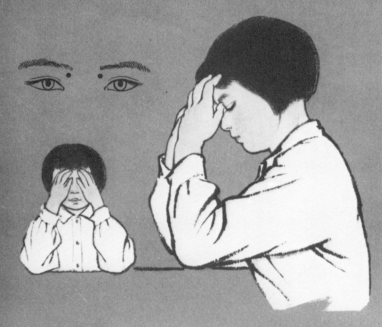

第一节　揉天应穴(拈竹下三分)

闭目静坐,以左右大拇指罗纹面按左右眉头下上眶角处,其他四指散开弯曲如弓状,支持在前额上,按揉面不要大(节拍8×8)。

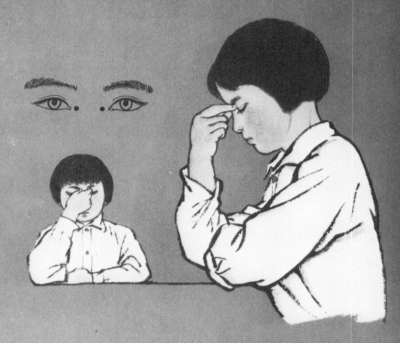

第二节　挤按睛明穴

以左手或右手大拇指与食指挤按鼻根,先向下按,然后向上挤,一按一挤共一拍(节拍8×8)。

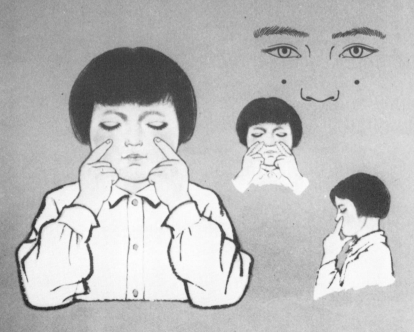

第三节　揉四白穴

先以两手食指与中指并拢,放在紧靠鼻翼两侧,大拇指支撑在下颚骨凹陷处,然后放下中指,在面颊中央部按揉(节拍8×8)。

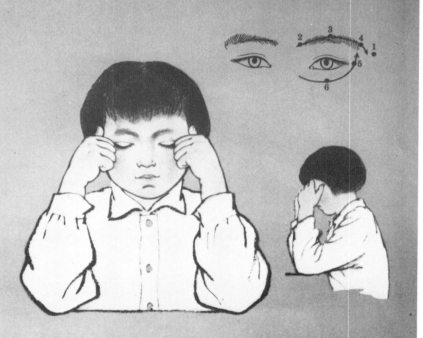

第四节　按太阳穴轮刮眼眶(太阳、拈竹、鱼腰、丝竹空、瞳子髎(liáo)、承泣等穴)

拳起四指,以左右大拇指罗纹面按太阳穴,以左右食指第二节内侧面轮刮眼眶上下一圈,先上后下,轮刮上下一圈计四拍(节拍8×8)。

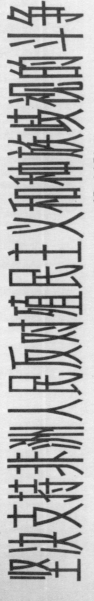

坚决支持非洲人民反对殖民主义和种族歧视的斗争

Resolutely Support the Struggle of the African People Against Colonialism and Racial Discrimination

Soutenons résolument les peuples d'Afrique dans leur lutte contre le colonialisme et la discrimination raciale!

不可抗拒的历史潮流

国家要独立 民族要解放 人民要革命

Irresistible Historical Trend
Countries Want Independence, Nations Want Liberation, the People Want Revolution
Le courant de l'histoire est irrésistible
Les pays veulent l'indépendance, les nations veulent la libération, et les peuples veulent la révolution

中国上海人民出版社出版 Published by the Shanghai People's Publishing House, Shanghai, China
中国国际书店发行 Distributed by Guoji Shudian (China Publications Centre), Peking, China 84 CBE—82m

团结起来 争取更大的胜利

学 英 雄 精 神　走 英 雄 道 路

延 安 新 春

纪念"二七"大罢工五十周年
（1923——1973）

手握手中铁，工人颈上血，须可折，肢可裂，
奋斗的精神不消灭！劳苦的群众们，快起来团结！

《京汉铁路工人歌》

要 把 无 产 阶 级 文 化 大 革 命 进 行 到 底

军民联防 铁壁铜墙

IRON BASTION—JOINT DEFENCE BY THE ARMY AND THE PEOPLE

UNE MURAILLE INDESTRUCTIBLE—DEFENSE CONJOINTE
PAR L'ARMEE POPULAIRE DE LIBERATION ET LE PEUPLE

FEST WIE EIN STÄHLERNES BOLLWERK STEHT DIE VEREINIGTE
VERTEIDIGUNGSGRUPPE VON ARMEE UND VOLK

工农兵是批林批孔的主力军

提高警惕 加强练兵

苦练杀敌本领

展翅

雏鹰

学习人民 为人民

纪念"南京路上好八连"命名十周年

敬爱的周恩来总理永远和我们在一起

狠批"四人帮" 掀起工业学大庆农业学大寨新高潮

节 日 的 水 乡

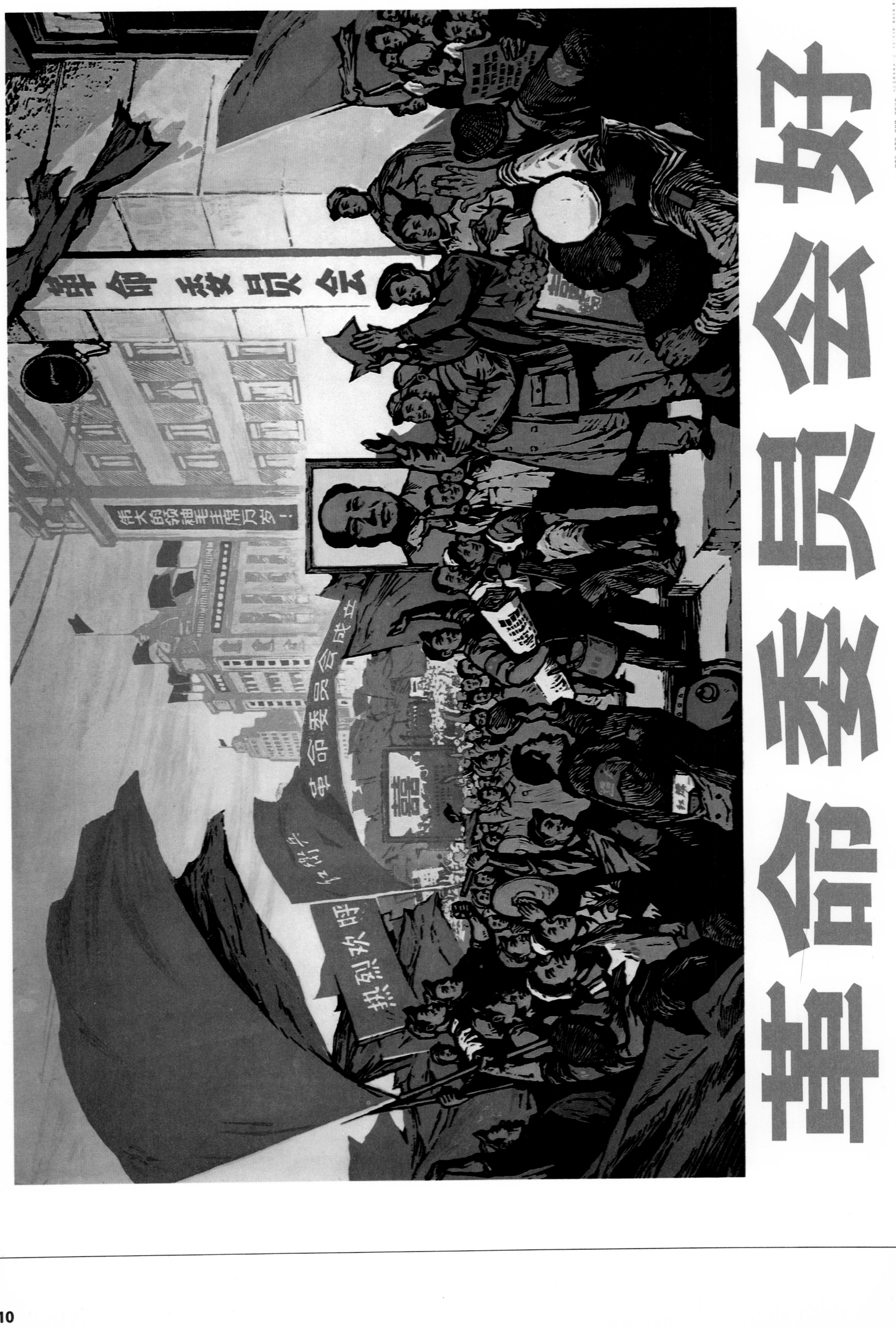
革命委员会好
革命委员会
伟大的领袖毛主席万岁！
热烈欢呼
革命委员会成立
红卫兵
喜

六亿神州尽舜尧

宋飞等 作　广东人民出版社出版　广东省新华书店发行　广东美术印刷厂印刷
1976年8月第一版　1976年8月第一次印刷　书号8111·1586　定价：0.14元